The B
Blu

Table of Contents

Chapter 1 – Introduction, Buy to Let Strategies and Finding a Suitable Investment..................7

    Introduction..............................8
    Your long term goals...........................10
    Risk vs reward.............................12
    Finding a suitable property...................14
    Looking for fundamentals....................16
    Viewing the property..........................18
    Houses vs flats...............................23
    Furnished vs unfurnished....................26
    Valuation / survey types.......................29
    Types of property investments..............31
    Family / professional lets.....................32
    Students..33
    HMOs..34
    DSS...35
    Buying/Owning through a limited company...................................36
    Holiday lets.......................................38
    Corporate lets...................................39
    Buy to let strategies...........................40
    Buy and Hold....................................40
    Capital growth vs rental income............41

Capital growth..................................42
Rental income..................................43
Let to Buy..45
Buying below market value and recycling your deposit..................................47
The costs of purchasing a buy to let......49

Chapter 2..54
Mortgage and Finance Options..................54
Mortgage Basics..............................55
Interest only vs Repayment Mortgages...57
Interest only mortgages.......................59
Fixed rate vs variable..........................60
Consumer BTL vs Investment Property Loan..62
How much can I borrow?........................64
Bridging finance................................66
Broker vs bank..................................67
Your Eligibility and Mortgage Criteria.....74
Own your own home............................74
First time landlords............................78
Minimum income requirement..............81
Your Age..84
Maximum Portfolio Size......................87
First Time Buyer Buy to Let..................90
Limited Company Buy to Lets................91

Minimum Time in UK..............................93
Visa Criteria..95
Maximum Number of Applicants..........98
Let to Buy...100
Sole Owner Joint Proprietor................104
Raising Capital without an Offer Accepted On a Buy to Let............................105
Minimum Loan Size / Minimum Property Value..108
Minimum/Maximum Term (Length of Mortgage).......................................110
Can Arrangement Fees Be Added Above Loan to Values............................112
How Long Are Mortgage Offers Valid For?...114
Studio Flats..116
How Many Years Need To Be Left On The Lease?..................................118
HMOs..121
How Tenant Types Can Affect Mortgages....................................123
Family Let / Professional Lets..............123
Student Lets / Larger Professional Lets On a Single AST..................................124
DSS...125
HMOs / Student Lets With Multiple Tenancy Agreements....................125
Remotgaging..126

Releasing Equity…………………………..127
Loan to Values………...……………………128

Chapter 3…………………………………….129
Management of your investment…………..129
How to Find Tenants………………………130
Traditional Methods…………………………133
Managing the Tenant Finding Process..134
Checks To Carry Out Prior To Letting Your Property…………………………………...135
Right to Rent Checks……………………..135
Deposit Protection Scheme……………...136
The Overall Safety of the Property……..137
Gas and Electrical Certificates………….137
Energy Performance Certificate (EPC)..138
A Detailed Inventory………………………138
The Tenancy Agreement…………………139
How to Manage Tenants…………………140
Management/Letting Agent vs Self-Management……………………………...140
Late Rental Payments……………………142
Eviction of Tenants………………………144
Managing Difficult Tenants……………..145
Your Responsibilities as a Landlord….146
Keep Your Property Safe………………..146

Gas and Electrical Appliances and Safety Checks..147
Smoke/Fire Alarms...............................147
Carrying out Repairs..........................148
Insurance...148
Buy to Let Tax....................................149
Rental Income....................................149
Stamp Duty..151
Tax Relief on Mortgage Interest..........153
Wear and Tear Allowance...................155
Capital Gains Tax...............................156
Insurance Available for Landlords.......157

Chapter 4 – Glossary..............................158

Chapter 1 – Introduction, Buy to Let Strategies and Finding a Suitable Investment

Introduction

Welcome to the 'The Buy To Let Blueprint'. First of all I would like to thank you for purchasing this guide, I have over a decade experience working and investing in the UK property market. I am aiming share all of my knowledge and experience and provide you with a step by step blueprint from finding a property, sourcing finance, managing your investment and expanding your property portfolio.

Property investment can be a powerful tool which can provide a passive income which can be passed through generations and create ongoing wealth for yourself and your family. In the guide we will discuss your possible strategies which you can implement and make your own blueprint whatever your long term goals may be.

With any investment there is potential risk and the property market can change very quickly, we will discuss the use of professionals throughout this guide so please always professional advice on current conditions in the marketplace and use this blueprint as an overview.

So why property? Why not another form of investment? I think the major benefit of property investment in comparison to stocks, shares, currencies etc. is you will own a physical asset (the property) which can be used to provide a potentially passive income. If the price of a share reduces you will be left with very little to show for it; however with property you will always have an asset that everyone needs (a home). Although property prices can decrease as we seen in 2008/2009 historically the value of property has always increased in the long term. Depending on your strategy you should see property investment as a long term investment, you will have rental voids and you may have bad tenants however over the course of 20, 25, 30 years these inconveniences will simply be inconveniences and you should view property investment not as a 'get rich scheme' but as a long term asset that you will be able to pass through generations.

I have designed this blueprint so you will be able to look up specific details in regard to anything buy to let at short notice or you can simply sit back, start from page one and start planning your property portfolio.

Your long term goals

Before you go out and find out a suitable investment it is worth thinking about your long term goals. Property investment has almost unlimited possibilities and everyone will have different goals, aspirations, levels of risk you are willing to undertake and ambitions. You may just want to make a few extra £100's every month or you maybe you want to retire early, with property investment this is definitely possible and you may be surprised how easily it can be done.

I am a firm believer in setting goals, throughout my life I have set goals, such as graduating from university, getting a job, buying my first flat and purchasing my first investment. Although the previously mentioned goals may not seem like marvellously big goals, they are all however positive targets which will ultimately provide me with a better lifestyle which translates into other areas of my life. When setting goals it is important that they are SMART (although there are other theories). But what are SMART goals? They are Specific, Measurable, Achievable, Realistic and Trackable.

In regard to Buy to Let a SMART could be:

Specific – I want to purchase a two bedroom flat which I will let out in the Newham borough of London. It is important that you are very specific. If you are too vague the goal will almost seem unobtainable and you may struggle to focus on the goal.

Measurable – You will want to measure your progress and with property investment. This can be an easy one as it will either be your name on the deeds or lease or not. Other than the number of properties you own you can also measure the amount of rental income you receive.

Achievable- It is important your goal is achievable; there isn't much point in setting a goal where you will own a property portfolio which provides an income of £10,000 per month in the next six months if you don't have a deposit in place to begin with. You should assess the assets you have available (which we will discuss in more depth shortly) and figure out what is achievable.

Realistic – Similar to achievable it is worth considering if you goal is realistic so if you have a partner, three children and a full time job do you really have the time to manage 10 HMO properties all by yourself? Being realistic is more about time management and hopefully this will influence your strategy when it comes to buy to let.

Trackable – Trackable in SMART goals means you will be able to track your goal and set deadlines for accomplishing it. At the beginning of your property journey it may take several years in order you for to purchase your first property which is completely fine, but with the additional income from your first purchase it will hopefully take less time to purchase your next.

Risk vs reward

With any investment there is potential risk and throughout the blueprint we will discuss risk vs reward. It is possible to have a very 'hands off' portfolio where your tenants will typically go to work, pay their rent on time very month and look after the property. Although this scenario sounds idyllic, you may not receive the same rewards in comparison to a portfolio of HMO properties or student lets which can attract a higher return on investment. There is no right or wrong answers to risk vs reward and it all comes down to your personal preference and attitude to risk.

I would always look at a worst case scenario, what if the property wasn't let out for a prolonged period of time; will you be able to afford the mortgage payments? It is very important to look at what assets you have available and also your income going forward. I would thoroughly recommend downloading a spreadsheet from the internet to work out exactly how much you have at the end of each month after your mortgage/bills/childcare are taken care of. You do not want to be in position (at least initially) that you are solely relying on rental income to cater for your needs because one part of any property investment is the potential risk that the property is not let out and not producing an income.

One part of buy to let which is often overlooked is the ongoing maintenance of the property, you will be responsible for the general upkeep of the property and if the boiler breaks you will be responsible for replacing it. Certain types of tenant will probably costs more in ongoing maintenance, such as student lets where you may have to spend a few thousand every year to get the property back to a suitable standard for the coming academic year.

One very good way to mitigate risk is with insurance, there are numerous types of insurance policies available to landlords which we will discuss in more depth later in the blueprint, but spending a little every month can save you a lot when you need it.

It is worth mentioning you may never find an absolutely perfect investment which combines both high rental yield and high capital growth. Typically an investment will fail into two main categories, your investment may benefit from the value of the increasing a lot over time (for example in London) or your property will produce a high rental yield but not benefit from 5-10% growth in value each year (for example in the North East of England). Both of these strategies can carry their own challenges and risks but it is possible to find a property that provides a little of both and this is arguably the least risky option.

Finding a suitable property

There are over 25 million properties in the UK and to begin with, you will need to select one to begin your investment journey. With potentially millions of options available it can be very difficult to select just one. This section of the blueprint will provide you with some tips and hopefully you will be able to narrow down your search and choose the correct property for you.

Research, research, research

"He who fails to prepare, should prepare to fail". Research and knowledge is the cornerstone of any investment, this is perhaps the most important part. I would treat any buy to let purchase similar to a purchase a residential property for myself and my family to live in. As previously mentioned, there will be risks and if you complete the research to the best of your ability you should be able to mitigate some potential downfalls.

Location, location, location

We have all seen the television show, but location is paramount when it comes to buy to let investment. In 2016, the average house price in the UK increased by 7.2% which definitely beats any ISA available today. You can maximise this capital growth by buying in an up and coming area. In 2016, the area with the highest capital growth was Luton at a staggering 19.4%, this is due to the increase in previous years of property prices in London and Luton having great commuting infrastructure to the Capital. So it is best to thoroughly research the area you are looking to purchase in. Great tools to use are Zoopla, Right Move and also the Land Registry to find out exactly how much property has sold for in a particular area. Some estate agents (but not all) will advertise property at above market value in anticipation for future negotiations with buyers or to secure the sale in comparison to other agents who may initially value the property for less. It is also important to check out your competition, you can do this by simply looking at properties very similar to your potential investment and looking for properties that are 'let agreed', but bear in mind that 'let agreed' is not always the exact price that has been advertised. When considering location, it is always worth looking for great fundamentals which we will discuss in more depth in the next section.

Looking for fundamentals

When purchasing a buy to let property, it is important you purchase a property with great fundamentals. Fundamentals are things that make any area somewhere people will want to live. As I am sure you will be aware, facilities such as shops, schools and other amenities can be very important. But I think probably the most important fundamental is places of employment. There are some remote areas in the UK with very little places of work nearby. Often areas with large employers near will have employees who may only live there a few days a week which can be great for smaller, lower cost properties.

If you are looking to target the family market it is worth considering which schools are in the catchment area for the property. I have heard of families simply renting a property in order for their children to attend a certain school. Also parks and local shops can be great fundamentals for this market.

If you are looking at potentially a HMO (a house of multiple occupation) then the actual location and the fundamentals surrounding the property will be crucial. Often this type of property is let to young professionals and I have heard of some landlords buying slightly cheaper properties with slightly worse fundamentals and they have struggled to keep the property fully tenanted.

Similar to HMOs, with the student market, it is very important to have great fundamentals. I was once a student and similar to most students today I wanted my home to be within walking distance to my university, the city centre and also shops. Again, if the property is slightly too far away you may struggle to let the property at its full potential.

It is very important to picture your ideal tenant and think about when you were a student, young professional, starting a family or coming up to retirement, what exactly would you want nearby? A very important factor is also who lives in the area. Most students for example will want to live near younger people and be within walking to their friends and some families will probably not want to live next door to a group of students who enjoy playing music or having their friends over. I would advise to picture yourself in your tenants shoes as fundamentals can make or break any investment.

Viewing the property

When you find a potential Buy to Let investment, you have checked there are good fundamentals and you feel the property may be a good investment then it is time to view the property. Often investors think that since they will not living there this isn't too important, but remember you are potentially going to pay £100k's. I would advise to treat he viewing as if you were going to view a property that you were to live in, if you wouldn't want to live there, why would someone else? Similar to obtaining a residential mortgage, most mortgage lenders will allow you to upgrade from a basic valuation to more depth survey but always seek professional advice from a qualified surveyor to find out which level of survey will be the most appropriate (we will discuss this shortly).

Different times of day

If you are not local to the area it is important to consider what the area is like at different times of day. If you feel brave enough, it is probably best to have a walk around the area in the evening/night time. You will have some tenants who will do the same; if the property has been on the market for a while it could potentially be noisy neighbours next door in the evenings.

Who lives next door?

Probably the most common question a tenant will ask is who lives next door? In the majority of cases it will be a normal person who will probably be at work during the day and will go about their lives in a normal routine. If you could potentially find out their name and what they do for a living this will help when you come to let the property as it will put any potential tenants mind at rest that they are not moving next door to someone undesirable.

What is included?

It is important to treat the purchase as an investment and the whole idea of this is to make money. It is very important to ask if any furniture or appliances are included in the sale and have a good look at the quality of what is potentially included and think if it will be suitable for your type of tenant. If something is old or needs to be replaced don't be scared to ask the vendor to remove the item on completion of the sale, you don't want to spend the equivalent of a month's rent removing unwanted heavy furniture. If the vendor is offering to leave furniture you can potentially ask for a discount on the purchase price if this is not needed.

Bring a friend or trusted acquaintance

If this is your first investment it can be very rewarding (both financially and you may learn a thing or two) by taking a friend or someone you trust to get a second opinion. If you do know someone who has experience as a landlord they may be able to give you some expert insight into your specific area or investment type.

Has the property ever been tenanted?

This question can open up to a lot of potential conversations and may give you a better indication of what works for this property and what doesn't. If the property has been let out in the past, don't be afraid to ask what the rental income was because this may be different to what an estate may say.

Potential for future investment

Depending on your type of investment, you could benefit from additional rental income by adding an additional bedroom. Some simple possibilities could be change the layout of the property or by splitting a larger bedroom into two or you could potentially look to extend the property. A very common improvement is to convert an attic into an additional bedroom which can provide additional rental income.

Questions to ask when viewing a property?

When you are viewing a property there are literally thousands which can be asked, please see below some questions that may be relevant to your investment:

- How many viewings has the property had?
- Have you received any offers?
- What type of person/family has been viewing the property? (This can help with marketing your property)
- Why are you selling?
- Is there designated parking, if not, where is best to park?
- When was the property last re-wired?
- What condition is the roof in?
- How long is the lease? (if applicable)
- What is the council tax band?
- Who lives next door?

- Is there any insurance certificates you will provide for work that has been carried out and are you willing to provide them on completion?
- Will the existing tenant (if applicable) be willing to sign a new tenancy agreement?
- Are any of the neighbouring properties let out?
- Does the property have good mobile phone reception?
- Does the property have good internet connectivity?
- Has the property ever suffered from Japanese Knotweed?
- Has the property ever suffered from subsidence or heave?
- Can the property been renovated
- How much is the ground rent / service charge? (if applicable)
- What is included in the sale?
- Is the seller part of a chain?
- Can you provide a EPC (Energy Performance Certificate)
- Are there any disputes with the neighbours?
- Have the current tenants been in arrears in the past? (if applicable)

Houses vs flats

Houses vs flats is an age long question when it comes to property investment, some investors swear by houses and some by flats. Both have pros and cons and there is no right or wrong answer. The majority of investors who own multiple properties own both as this will diversify your portfolio.

The advantages of a house

Probably the biggest benefit of purchasing a house is you will not have any neighbours upstairs or downstairs. Having neighbours in close proximity can sometimes cause issues and end up taking more of your time managing the investment. Another major benefit of purchasing a house is in the majority of cases you will also own the freehold for a property. By owning the freehold you will also own the area the property sits upon and also the surrounding land. When owning the freehold for a property, you will essentially own the land forever, you will not need anyone else's permission (in exception to planning permission if applicable) to adjust or extend the property.

The disadvantages of a house

Before you run out and purchase a house there a few downsides, first of all you will be responsible for the structure of the property, although this is also true of flats, at least with flats, you will share this responsibility with the other flat owners in the building. Also, typically speaking a house in the same area will cost more than a flat, so if you are solely looking to purchase property in a specific area you may struggle to expand your portfolio at the same speed in comparison to purchasing flats. It is also worth considering that the start-up costs for a house can be more expensive such as stamp duty, mortgage interest and also the overall maintenance for a house can be more expensive (due to houses typically being bigger than flats). One big disadvantage of a house is that they typically provide a lower rental yield in comparison to flats.

The advantages of a flat

As briefly mentioned, flats typically provide a higher rental yield and on paper this may make them a better investment and overall the running and maintenance costs can be cheaper also. With a lower cost of entry you should be able to expand your portfolio quicker which over the long term can allow you to generate wealth quicker. Over the past decade, flats have outgrown houses in terms of capital growth, although this may change in the future, but buying the right flat in the right area can be a better return on investment when the property is sold.

The disadvantages of a flat

There a few disadvantages to flats to consider, probably the main one is turnover of tenants, depending on the area you buy in and your type of tenant, flats typically attract younger people who in a few years' time may want to start a family (and move into a house) or they move away leaving you with an empty property. With the majority of flats in England and Wales there will be a lease on the property which will ultimately one day expire. At the end of the lease the property will return to the freeholder, this is not too much of an issue if the lease is 999 years but if the lease is below 85 years the value of the property may decrease every few years because you may have to pay potentially thousands to get the lease extended. Depending on the flat, you may have to pay ground rent and a service charge which will eat into your rental income so whenever you view a flat always ask how much this cost is every month and calculate this into your monthly outgoings.

Furnished vs unfurnished

Letting a property on a furnished or unfurnished basis will massively depend on the type of tenant you are looking to attract. For example if we look at a student let, a large number of students move to a new city to attend university. Relocation costs can be very expensive (especially for students or young people). The last thing most students will want to spend money on is a bed, wardrobes, living room furniture etc. so by offering the basics included in your rental property should attract more tenants and you can also charge extra in rent. By spending even a few hundred pounds on some decent second hand furniture can work out to be an excellent investment as after your tenant has moved out you will still own the furniture which can be sold or re-used for a new tenant. Depending on your type of tenant I would advise to be cautious in regard to the amount you spend on furniture, if you are looking to invest in a student let or a HMO you should typically expect to have a high level of wear and tear and we have all heard of tenants who have purposely destroyed or even stolen expensive furniture/fittings from a property. There are advantages and disadvantages to both and by speaking to a local agent they should be able to provide with the best advice which will let your property out the quickest to right tenant.

The advantages of letting a furnished property

As previously mentioned, you can often charge a higher rent; this is because a tenant will save money on furnishing the property which can lead to a quicker amount of time to find a suitable tenant. If you are creative or know someone who is, then you can 'stage' the property. A lot of people when entering an empty home may lack imagination and simply see five or six empty rooms and immediately want to move onto their next viewing, we will discuss this in more detail later in the blueprint. You will also own an asset (the furniture) which as mentioned can be used multiple times and sold or donated to charity if you no longer need it any more.

The advantages of letting an unfurnished property

If you target tenant is a family who will probably already own their own furniture, if you fill a property will furniture this will more than likely deter tenants from renting from you or you may be left with unwanted items that can be expensive to get rid of. By targeting your market correctly you will save your time, money and effort which are probably the three most important things with any investment. One very big advantage of letting a property unfurnished is you will not have to worry about the state you will receive your £500 sofa in in 12 months' time. Also, you will not be a position where if a new tenants asks for the property to be unfurnished you will not have to pay for removal or storage costs.

Valuation / survey types

If you are purchasing a property with a mortgage then every mortgage lender will carry out a valuation of the property. The valuation is to essentially ensure the property is adequate security for the mortgage and they will not be in negative equity if they have to repossess. Most mortgage lenders will require a basic valuation to be carried out but you can opt to upgrade this basic valuation to a more in-depth survey at an additional cost which can provide peace of mind in regard to potential issues the property may have.

Basic valuation

A basic valuation as the name suggest is very basic, some mortgage lenders will not even physically view the property, they may use an 'indexed valuation' which means they look at a data-base and assess the value on that or they may do a 'drive-by valuation' where they get a surveyor to drive past the property and base the value on that. If the lender does decide to do an internal inspection they will mainly only look for any structural movement or any other major potential defects or simply provide what they believe the property to be valued at and provide no further information.

Homebuyer's survey

A homebuyers survey is a lot more detailed than a basic valuation, typically the surveyor will look at certain areas of the property and mark them either green (this is ok) amber (this requires attention or red (this requires immediate attention). Depending on the age of the property I would always recommend to go with at least a homebuyers report (or equivalent) to get a second pair of eyes on the property. Overall the homebuyers report is a visual inspection of the property and there is potential that the surveyor may miss something.

Full building survey

A full building survey is the most thorough type of survey and this type of survey will probably not be the most appropriate for some properties (especially newer ones). As you can probably expect the full building survey is often the most expensive and the idea is they will look at literally everything, if something is missed you may have potential to claim against the firm who has carried the survey out.

As a landlord you will be responsible for the upkeep of the property (which we will discuss in depth later) but by paying a few hundred pounds you could potentially save yourself thousands if the boiler breaks!

Types of property investments

Before you view any properties or make any decisions, you will need to think of the type of property you will purchase and the type of tenant you will let the property too.

If this is your first investment, most landlords may purchase a property that can be let to a families, couples or professionals. These types of tenants will usually pay their rent on time, look after the property and are generally long term stable tenants. If you are looking for a long term, steady, generally low risk investment this may be the best option for you. Due to this investment being generally low risk, the amount of income you can receive may be limited.

If you are looking to make a higher yield on your rental income, then you can look to let your property as a house of multiple occupation (HMO), let to students or to tenants who are in receipt of housing benefit. These options are generally higher risk and may take a lot of more time and effort to set up and manage. We will discuss these options in a lot more depth in the next section.

Family / professional lets

Letting to a working family or professionals (for example a working couple or single person) is the most common type of tenancy in the UK. This is because this type of tenant is likely to pay their rent on time and look after your property. I have friends and family who have successfully let properties to a single family or professional for over a decade without any major issues. If you are looking for a 'hands off' investment with potentially very little work needed this may the best type of tenant for you. Due to this type of investment being relatively risk free the rewards can be limited in comparison to some of the other tenancy types we will discuss. It is also worth mentioning the term 'professional' is not limited to doctors, solicitors, etc. this term generally also includes anyone who is working. For first time landlords this is often the best recommended type of investment because you can learn so much and gain a lot of experience.

Students

Letting a property to students can be very profitable, the main advantage is you can let each bedroom on an individual basis whereas with a family or professionals you let the property as a single unit. Location is paramount if you are looking to purchase a student let. I was once a student and typically students will want to live near their friends (other students). If you purchase a property that is slightly out of the main student area you may struggle to fill the entire property. One of the most profitable options with student lets to purchase a house as you will be able to let the downstairs living room/dining room as an additional bedroom. When marketing a student let, timing is vital, most students look for properties between January/February in anticipation for the following academic year (starting in September). It is possible to successfully find tenants later in the year but the prime time is definitely earlier in the year. When it comes to obtaining a mortgage, most mainstream lenders will be ok with students, however they often have a maximum of 4/5 students and they will have to all be on one single assured tenancy agreement. Managing a student let (especially one with first year students) may involve a lot more time and you may have to deal with noise complaints from the neighbours etc. it is also worth budgeting towards an annual refurb of the property as you will experience more wear and tear.

HMOs

A HMO is a 'house of multiple occupancy'; similar to a student let, typically a HMO will be a larger house however each bedroom or unit will be let on separate tenancy agreements. The major benefit of a HMO is you can let rooms separately, so when a tenant moves out you will be able to replace them without having to market a full property to a family (for example). Due to having the flexibility to rent rooms out separately you can often receive a higher rental yield in comparison to a property let to a single person/family. When it comes to getting a mortgage, you will be limited with options and you will typically pay a higher rate of interest as HMOs are deemed more risky. The overall management of a HMO can be a lot more time consuming and expensive when it comes to maintaining the property which is why a lot of mortgage lenders require their potential customers to have previous experience as a landlord.

DSS

DSS is a now a defunct government agency which previously stood for 'Department of Social Security' and was a department of government which provided people with housing benefit. Although the Department of Social Security no longer exists it is still a term used by a lot of landlords/letting agents in regard to tenants who are in receipt of housing benefit. Although often unfairly stigmatised, this group of tenants do have a reputation of non-payment of rent and can be a risky investment. A way of decreasing the risk in regard to receiving rental income is to arrange for the rent to be paid to yourself direct instead of being paid direct to your tenant or to ask for a guarantor.

Buying/Owning through a limited company

As some of you will be aware (those of you who are not, we will discuss this later in the book) there is big tax changes happening in the buy to let market at the moment. One of the biggest being that mortgage/loan interest will no longer be classed an expense, as of tax year 2020/21 you will no longer be able to claim any relief for this business expenditure. A lot of landlords are now looking at transferring their portfolio's into limited companies but there are a few things to be aware of.

Technically the company which you set up will own the property however you will have to sign a personal guarantee. When obtaining a mortgage the lender will look at you as an individual, so you will personally have to meet the lenders criteria as will the company. The most common type of company for a buy to let is known a 'SPV' (Special purpose vehicle). Your SVP will be specifically set up to own and let out residential property and with most lenders will need your company will have to one of three SIC codes, they are 68100, 68209 and 68320. The company SIC code is essentially the purpose for the business and you will be asked for this when you set up your company via Companies House. It is important to mention most lenders will not allow you to use a company which trades in any other business, so for example if you are a self-employed builder who trades through a limited company you will not be able to use this company, you will have to set up a SPV.

Although at the moment this is quite a niche area of buy to let, in the future this may become common place as mortgage lenders need to lend in order to make a profit. Currently there are no 'high street' lenders which lend in this area and presently you will have to look at lenders such as Paragon, Precise and Aldermore who often charge higher rates of interest. So it is vital to speak to an accountant or tax adviser to consider if the higher amount of interest you will pay for this type of investment will offset the amount of tax payable.

If you are looking to 'transfer' an existing property from your personal name into a limited company this can be quite expensive. You will need to unfortunately need to hire two separate solicitors as the transfer will be classed a sale and other taxes such as capital gains and stamp duty may be applicable.

Holiday lets

A holiday let is essentially a property that is owned with the intention of letting for short periods of time to people who are enjoying a week or weekend away. Holiday lets can be very lucrative although you do need to own the correct type of property in the best location. Often you will receive a high, medium and low rental income depending on the time of year and it is important to factor in potential voids. The management of a holiday let can often be a lot more time consuming in comparison to a standard buy to let, as you will have to manage bookings, cancelations and cleaning/maintenance of the property. When it comes to financing a holiday let you will be restricted with options with only a few building Societies and specialist lenders are lending in this area (which we will discuss in more detail later in the book).

Corporate lets

A corporate let is quite similar to a standard buy to let, however instead of letting to a person you will let the property to a company. This company may use the property for their employees to stay over but typically meetings or other business activities will not be carried out there. Again, if you do decide to proceed down this path you will be limited with finance options but it is possible to secure a mortgage on this type of investment. The major benefit of a corporate let is that typically the length of a tenancy agreement can be a lot longer than a standard agreement (often 12-60 months) and typically the property will be looked after because what type of company would want their staff to stay somewhere unclean or not looked after.

Buy to let strategies

When you begin your adventure into Buy to Let it is very important to consider what your long term plans are. We have previously discussed setting goals, but you will also need a blueprint of how you are going to get there. There are numerous strategies when it comes to letting residential properties and you may see yourself using a combination of the ones we will discuss.

Buy and Hold

Buy and Hold' is probably the most common strategy as this will eliminate a lot of risk. Historically property prices in the UK have increased over the long term; there have been instances for example in 2008 when prices dramatically fell, however over the long term property prices have increased. So even if we do see a repeat of the recession of 2008, if you are able to keep a hold of the property then historically speaking, one day the value of this investment will rise.

This strategy is extremely popular because you will not need to do much, apart from manage your tenants and remortgage your property every few years. Due to this strategy being quite 'hands off' and the risk being reduced, this is reflected the potential rewards you can receive.

Capital growth vs rental income

Capital growth is essentially the amount in value that you expect the property to increase by in the future, whereas rental income (or yield) is the amount of rental income you expect to receive in comparison to the property value. Typically in the South East of England (especially London) the amount of rental income vs the value of the property tends to a lot less than in the North of England and other parts of the UK (and vice-versa).

It is important to think about what you would like to gain from the investment, if you are looking for additional income now, if you purchase a property in London this may not be the best option, but if you are planning to 'buy and hold' and eventually sell to benefit from the capital growth then the South East of England may be the best option.

Capital growth

The main risk with capital growth is there is potential the property may not increase in value, or at least at the level you expect. Also, if you are looking to take out a buy to let mortgage the amount you will be able to borrow will usually be dictated by the rental income you receive. So you may have a property that is worth £500,000 and you may be looking to borrow 75% of this (£375,000) however you may need a rental income of £2,492 every month or potentially higher depending on the lender (check out the mortgage section for how this calculation has been worked out). Often, people with high value properties will struggle to borrow the amount they are looking for, however this strategy can be very 'hands off' as you simply just need to 'buy and hold'. It is also worth taking into account when a second property is sold (a property that is not your main residence), there may be capital gains tax payable, this is usually worked out on the original price you paid for the property and the price you sell the property, so this is definitely worth taking into account.

Rental income

When taking into account a property's rental income, a simple calculation can be carried out to easily compare investments. This calculation is worked out pre-tax (gross) due to induvial circumstances being different.

The calculation is simply:

Monthly rent multiplied by 12 months, divided by the property's value and multiplied by 100 = gross yield.

For example, if you receive £600/month in rent x 12 months = £7,200, your property's value is £130,000, £7,200 divided by £130,000 = 0.055, multiplied by 100 = 5.5%

The above calculation does not take into expenses or tax, if you want to look at a properties net yield, then the calculation is as follows:

Monthly rent multiplied 12 months, minus expenses and tax, divided by the property's value and multiplied by 100 = net yield.

For example, if you receive £600/month in rent x 12 months = £7,200, you have £2,400 in expenses and tax, £7,200 minus £2,400 = £4,800, your property's value is £130,000, £4,800 divided by £130,000 = 0.036, multiplied by 100 = 3.6%.

Even 3.6% as a yield is not a bad return when we consider we live in a world of record low interest rates. However, if you decide to purchase a property with a high yield, historically you may not benefit from much capital growth. There are certain areas of the UK where you can purchase a terrace house for as little as £40,000 and expect a rental income in excess of £400/month which can provide a gross yield in excess of 12%. However there is a risk, typically the type of tenant you may let too may not pay their rent every month, may be difficult to manage and may not look after the property, so this type of investment could be more costly to manage, (for example paying for repairs), you may have a high turnover of tenants and it may more difficult to sell if needed. When it comes to obtaining a mortgage on this type of property, you may be limited with options, typically the absolute minimum value of a buy to let property is around £40,000 but most lenders will need the value to be between £50,000 -£75,000 (we will discuss this in more depth later).

Overall, it is probably best to look for a property that is somewhere in between. But this will also be reflected the amount of profit you may receive from your investment.

Let to Buy

Let to Buy has been a very good strategy in the past and is quite an easy strategy to understand. 'Let to Buy' is basically letting out your existing property and potentially releasing equity to use to towards a deposit for a new property for yourself to live in, while still owning your previous home as a Buy to Let. Changes in stamp duty have made this strategy more expensive but if you plan to own the investment for a long period of time then this strategy can be very lucrative. The most important part of a let to buy is your existing home which will be turned into a rental property. If you have a mortgage on your current home then you will need at least 25% of equity within the property in order to remortgage it onto a buy to let basis, so if your property is valued at £100,000 then your mortgage balance will need to be £75,000 as a maximum. If your current mortgage balance is less than 75% of the current value of the property then you may potentially be able to borrow up to 75% loan to value and use the additional equity for a deposit on your new home. The amount you can borrow on the buy to let mortgage will be subject to the rental income you will receive (we will discuss this in more depth later) so it is important to speak to a good mortgage broker who can find a suitable lender for this type of transaction. When it comes to the onward purchase you may need to have a higher deposit than the 5% minimum needed.

The best way to facilitate a let to buy is to aim for 'simultaneous completion' so your Buy to Let mortgage and your onward residential purchase will complete on the same day. This will mean you will apply for both mortgages at the same time and you will need an offer accepted on your new residential property prior to any mortgage applications.

The major benefit of a Let to Buy is you will have previously lived in the Buy to Let property so you will know the property very well which can make it easier to market and if anything goes wrong in the property (such as boiler not working properly) you may be able to provide your tenant with advice on this. When you move into your new property you can make improvements to the property to add value so when you come to 'Let to Buy' again it may be quicker to achieve a higher market value for your Buy to Let remortgage.

This strategy has been very successful in the past but can be quite risky, especially if you are remortgaging your Buy to Let properties up to 75% loan to value because if the properties drop in value then you may be stuck with a portfolio you are unable to re-finance with high street lenders. As of April 2015 you will also have to pay an additional 3% in stamp duty for your onward residential properties.

Buying below market value and recycling your deposit

This strategy is often used by landlords who want to expand their portfolio by 'recycling' their deposit. This is essentially buying a property usually with something wrong with it such a short lease or a property in need of repair. The idea is you extend the lease or refurbish the property and then remortgage the property after a period of time for the full market value and release the equity you have gained.

For example, you purchase a flat with 60 years remaining the lease; you purchase this property for £200,000 with a 75% loan to value mortgage (£150,000 mortgage). You then extend the lease and now the property is worth £275,000. You may then be able to remortgage the property again at 75% loan to value which will provide you a mortgage of £206,250. You use £150,000 to replace the existing mortgage you will have £56,250 to use towards your next purchase (minus any costs for a lease extension and potential legal/tax implications).

It is also worth bearing in mind that you will often need to own the property for at least six months before you are able to remortgage and you may need to own the property for a certain period of time before you are able to extend the lease.

The above example is very basic, but you get the idea. Because this strategy involves more work and the risks are potentially higher, then the rewards can also be higher, but please consult professionals before embarking on any investment such as this.

If you are looking to buy a property that has something wrong with it then you may struggle to obtain a standard Buy to Let mortgage. There are other forms of finance available such as bridging finance which is designed to allow you to purchase a property and repay the finance quickly although this is often more expensive than a standard mortgage (we will discuss in more depth later in the book).

The costs of purchasing a buy to let

When it comes to financing your investment is it very important to budget every cost you will pay out initially. This in this section we will delve into all of the costs you will have to pay so hopefully you will not be surprised with any unexpected costs. We will look at the typical costs for a property valued at £100,000.

Deposit

As previously mentioned the typical deposit for a buy to let mortgage is 25% of the purchase price, so if you are buying a property for £100,000 then you will need to put down £25,000. It is possible to take out a mortgage with a 20% or even 15% deposit however you will be very limited with mortgage options and you will pay a higher rate of interest.

Solicitor/Conveyancing

Similar to a normal house purchase you will need a solicitor to carry out conveyancing work for your purchase. If you are buying a flat the costs for conveyancing do tend a little more expensive due to the additional legal work which needs to be carried out. The average cost for a solicitor will be £800 - £2,000. It is advisable to not instruct the cheapest the solicitor you can find because the work a solicitor carries out for any purchase is very important and often the quote you receive from the cheapest solicitor at the beginning may be different to the price you pay at the end.

Stamp duty

As we will discuss in more depth later in this book there has been drastic changes in stamp duty in recent years. If you currently own a residential property and you are purchasing a buy to let then you will need to pay an additional 3% in stamp duty on top of the standard charge. There are several very good calculators online where you can find out exactly how much you will pay.

Valuation/Survey fees

If you are obtaining a mortgage for your purchase then your mortgage lender will always carry a basic valuation to check the value of the property. The typical costs for this will be £0-£250. As previously discussed you will have the option to upgrade a basic valuation to a more in depth survey (a homebuyers or full building survey). Please see the chart which will give you a rough indication in regard to costs.

Property value	Basic Valuation	Homebuyers report	Full Structural Survey
£0 - £100,000	£0 - £250	£200 - £450	£500 - 700
£100,001 - £250,000	£0 - £350	£300 - £650	£550 - £800
£250,001 - £500,000	£0 - £500	£550 - £900	£750 - £1,250
£500,001 - £750,000	£0 - £650	£800 - £1,350	£1,000 - £1,750
£750,001 - £1,000,000	£0 - £800	£1,000 - £1,500	£1,250 - £2,250

| £1,000,001+ | £0 - £1,000+ | £1,500+ | £2,000+ |

Mortgage arrangement fees

Buy to let mortgages typically have higher arrangement fees than standard residential mortgages which can vary anywhere between £0 - £2,500. You will often have the option to add these fees to the mortgage but bear in mind that some mortgage lenders will not allow you to add fees above the mortgage products loan to value, so for example if you buying a property for £100,000 and you are borrowing £75,000 (75% LTV) and there is a £1,000 arrangement fee you will have to either pay this fee upfront or slightly decrease the amount you are borrowing by £1,000. I would always advise to decrease the amount you are borrowing and add the fee to the mortgage because sometimes arrangement fees are non-refundable and most mortgages will allow you to overpay by up to 10% of the balance so when the mortgage completes you can make an overpayment of £1,000 and you will mean you pay no interest on this fee.

Mortgage booking fees

Mortgage booking fees are slightly different to arrangement fees; they typically tend to be smaller than arrangement fees, often between £99 to £499. This fee normally is needed to be paid upfront and cannot be added to the mortgage. This fee is often charged by smaller lenders and is described to secure the rate but in reality it is protect the lender from working on cases that may fall through.

Renovation/Refurb Costs

If the property you are looking to purchase needs some work done it is important to get a professional to quote for the work that needs to be done prior to exchange of contracts (when the purchase becomes legally binding). This can costs anywhere from £0 - £100,000's+.

Example costs for a property valued at £100,000

Deposit - £25,000

Solicitor/Conveyancing - £1,500

Stamp Duty - £3,000

Valuation / survey - £450

Mortgage arrangement fees - £999

Mortgage booking fees - £99

Renovation/Refurb costs - £2,000

Total = £33,048

Chapter 2

Mortgage and Finance Options

Mortgage Basics

A buy to let mortgage is a financial product designed for purchasing and letting out residential property. The interest rates for buy to let mortgages typically depend to be higher than residential mortgages; this is due to a buy to let being designed for investment purposes and the risk is higher for the lender in comparison to a residential mortgage. A common misconception is you can take out a buy to let mortgage on commercial property or they can be used for flipping properties, but you will only be allowed to let residential properties so alternative forms of financial are available for that type of investment.

One of the biggest differences between buy to let and residential mortgages is you will typically need a 25% deposit. Almost all of the high street lenders will require this size of deposit, it is possible to obtain a buy to let mortgage with 20% or even a 15% deposit, however you will be limited with options and this will be reflected in the interest rate payable.

If you are looking to purchase an investment property and let it to a family member you will be limited with options. The buy to let mortgage market is mostly unregulated by the Financial Conduct Authority, but if you place a family member in the property, the mortgage will automatically become regulated so your mortgage lender will need to carry out an affordability assessment/meet other regulations and the mortgage will automatically become regulated.

This brings us to Affordability, typically most mortgage lenders will base the amount you can borrow on the rental income the property will generate (will discuss this is more depth later). Mortgage lenders do also like their customers to have a separate income that is not related to property investment which can be used to cover any potentially rental voids and ongoing maintenance. Typically most mortgage lenders will require you to have a £25,000 income through separate employment or self-employment.

Interest only vs Repayment Mortgages

One important decision you will need to make for your mortgage will be if you take your mortgage on a repayment or interest only basis. This decision will depend on your long term plans for the property. If you are looking to eventually own a mortgage free property which will produce an income, it may be best to put the mortgage on a repayment basis, or if you are looking to maximise your monthly income then an interest only mortgage may be the best option.

Unlike residential mortgages, buy to let lenders are a lot more relaxed when it comes to making this decision. Often with a residential mortgage you will need to demonstrate a credible repayment strategy for an interest only mortgage (for example an endowment, managed invest plan, sale of another property etc.) to pay back the interest only element. Whereas all buy to let lenders will accept sale of the mortgaged property as a repayment plan.

There are both advantages and disadvantages to each option and we will discuss these below.
Repayment

A repayment mortgage or a mortgage where you pay both interest and capital every month basically means that at the end of the term of the mortgage (assuming that the whole balance is on a repayment basis) you will have nothing else to pay. The major benefit of this type of mortgage is that every month you will see the balance of your mortgage reduce and you will have peace of mind that at the end of the mortgage term you will own a debt free asset. You will also pay less interest. The reason you will pay less interest is because almost all lenders in the

UK calculate their interest on a daily basis (this is in comparison to having an interest only mortgage and making no overpayments). In the olden days, lenders would calculate their interest on an annual basis meaning that they would review the amount of interest you pay once every year. For example if you have a £200,000 mortgage and your interest rate is 5%, when a lender reviews the interest on your mortgage on an annual basis you will pay £10,000 in interest over the course of the year (5% of £200,000 = £10,000). The £10,000 of interest you will pay will stay the same over the course of the year no matter how many payments you make. However with interest calculated on a daily basis, every month you will be reducing the £200,000 you have borrowed and the lender will re-calculate the interest they charge so assuming you keep up with repayments the amount of interest you pay will be less. The only bad side to repayment mortgage is the power of inflation but we will explore this in the next section.

Interest only mortgages

An interest only mortgage is where you literally only pay interest on the money you have borrowed, so if you borrow £200,000 you will only pay interest on this. So back to our previous example, if your interest rate is 5% then you will pay £10,000 in interest per annum, so a monthly payment of £833.33. Assuming you don't make any overpayments, you will still owe £200,000 at the end of your mortgage term.

The average house in the UK in 1990 was valued in the region of £60,000, over time with the power of inflation the value of money goes down, due to more money being pumped into the system. So back in 1990, depending on your circumstances £60,000 may been a lot of money or not much at all but I think we can all agree that you would rather pay £60,000 today in comparison to 1990. Basing figures on the Bank of England's website inflation calculator, £60,000 in 1990 is the equivalent of over £123,000 in today's money so by delaying payment of the full mortgage balance it really can work out cheaper to take out an interest only mortgage.

Other than inflation, the major advantage of an interest only mortgage is your monthly payments will be less per month. This can be especially helpful in regard to cash flow for your investment and also building your portfolio. The majority of landlords do have their mortgages on an interest only basis due to this reason, with the intention to sell the property at the end of the mortgage term or at retirement age to repay the amount borrowed.

Fixed rate vs variable

Other than repayment vs interest only a key decision you will have to make is fixed vs variable rates. Both have pros and cons and it will come down to your personal thoughts on the way interest rates are heading, your attitude to risk and your overall strategy.

The key advantage of a fixed rate mortgage is you will know exactly what you will pay each month which can be especially helpful when it comes to budgeting. Also with interest rates at record lows you can fix in at a very attractive rate and benefit from long term stable payments. The major disadvantage of a fixed rate is it can often be very expensive to exit a deal early so please think about your long terms plans with the property before fixing in for five years, also historically fixed rate mortgages do tend to be more expensive in comparison to variable rates.

If you feel rates will remain low or you are not 100% certain about your plans with the investment it may be the best option to opt for a variable rate mortgage. There are two main options you can pick from; the first is a tracker rate, which tracks the Bank of England base rate, so if the Base Rate moves your payment will too. The second option is a discount variable rate; this will often discount the lenders standard variable which can be risky as a lender could (in theory) change this at any time. The obvious risk with a variable rate is that your payments could change but you can sometimes benefit from a deal which has no exit fees so you will be free to redeem the mortgage or switch to a new lender at any point.

Consumer BTL vs Investment Property Loan

As of 2016, some new regulation came into the buy to let marketplace. Mortgage lenders now class every buy to let mortgage as either a 'consumer buy to let' (CBTL) or an 'investment property loan' (IPL).

Essentially a consumer buy to let is a customer who when they first purchased a property their intention was to not let the property out (for example they bought the property for a family member or they lived in the property). Whereas an investment property loan is designed for the potentially more experienced investor who plans to let the property out immediately.

The idea behind this distinction is to protect accidental landlords and potentially less experienced people from the currently unregulated buy to let market. Since the initial guidelines were introduced, unsurprisingly mortgage lenders have interpreted the rules differently. Thankfully the majority of buy to let lenders will treat CBTL and IPL exactly the same, however there are a few exceptions, certain lenders will not lend to consumer buy to let clients.

If you have lived in a property in the past/or currently and you would now like to convert the mortgage onto a buy to let basis there is a chance that a lender may class this as a consumer buy to let. Probably the biggest determining factor will be if you own another property that is let out. If you own another property (mortgaged or not) that is currently let out, then most buy to let mortgages you obtain will be now classed as an investment property loan as you will be seen as an experienced investor.

The most common scenario that can cause issues is when clients do a 'let to buy' (letting out your existing residential property then purchasing a new residential home). If you don't currently own another investment property then the chances are your buy to let mortgage will be treat as a CBTL.

By answering these questions you should be able to work out how a buy to let lender will class you as:

Are you a first time landlord?
Have you/or a family ever lived in the property in the past?
Do you own any other buy to let properties?

How much can I borrow?

As previously mentioned, the amount you can borrow on a Buy to Let mortgage will mainly depend on the rental income you will receive from the property. A typical calculation most lenders use is the following:

Loan amount – stress tested at 5.5% - multiplied by 145%.

The above calculation is an easy way of working out how much rental income you will need for an investment.

For example if you are looking to borrow £100,000, a mortgage lender will assume you are paying 5.5% as an interest rate, so on an interest only mortgage you will pay £5,500 over the course of 12 months (5.5% of £100,000 = £5,500). You will probably be paying a lot less as an interest rate, but mortgage lenders like to stress test this because interest rates may increase in the future, so what seems like a viable investment today may not be if interest rates increase.

If your mortgage lender is using 5.5% as a stress test, in our £100,000 mortgage example, a lender will assume you are paying £458.33 each month (£5,500 divided by 12 = £458.33). Then the mortgage lender will multiply the £458.33 by 145%, so you will need a rental income of £664.58 in order to borrow £100,000.

So to break this down, if you are looking to borrow £100,000, the lender will assume a rate of 5.5% this equals £458.33/month, then this figure is multiplied by 145% which equals a rental requirement of £665.58.

5.5% at 145% is typically the average that most high street lender use, however there are some lenders who have ammended this calculation slightly, for example one very big lender uses 5.5% at 125% which means you may be able to borrow more by looking at different lenders.

If the above figures are not working for your investment, don't worry, there is a small handful of mortgage lenders which can do what is called 'top slicing'. Top slicing is essentially when a mortgage lender also looks at your income from your employment or self-employed as well as the rental income. If your property will not produce enough rental income to borrow the amount you are looking for, then speaking to a good broker will definitely be a good option to consider.

Bridging finance

Bridging finance is a financial product designed to allow you to borrow money for a short period of time then repay the full amount without any penalty. Bridging finance is the perfect option if you are looking to 'flip' a property or buy at auction. It is very important to consider that bridging finance is very expensive, often around 1.5% per month, so if you borrowed £100,000 then you will pay £1,500 in interest per month.

If you are considering bridging finance there are two main options, closed or open bridging.

Closed bridging finance is when an induvial has a certain source of long finance lined up, such as mortgage which will be completing soon or the sale of a property. This form of finance is usually cheaper than open bridging due to the certainty of when the loan will be repaid.

Open bridging finance is when the borrower has no certain plan to repay the amount borrowed so the rates do tend to be higher. This option can be a lot more flexible and sometimes the term will have no end date but interest will continuously be charged.

When obtaining bridging finance it is important to think about your exist strategy, the most common types will be sale of property or remortgaging the property at a later date.

Broker vs bank

One very important decision you will need to make will be if you want to go direct to a bank for your mortgage or if you would prefer to speak to a broker. There are advantages and disadvantages of both. This decision will depend on your circumstances at the moment, how much spare time you have and how much control you would like over the process. Unlike residential mortgage lenders there is a large number of lenders who only deal with brokers so I would always advice to approach a broker to see what they can offer in comparison to what you may have found online.

Let's start with the advantages of going direct to a bank:

You may have more control - One of the biggest disadvantages of going through a broker is that they will be acting as a middle man between you and the bank. If you are speaking to a lender direct you may be able to give them a call for an update whenever you like, by going through a broker, you will need to phone them and they will need to call the lender and then they will call you back. This process can take a longer to find out what is going on as your broker will probably have dozens of other cases they are working on and their priority when you call may be not be to drop everything and call the lender to get you can update.

It may be quicker - This is not always guaranteed and will massively depend on how quickly you can provide documents that the lender requires and the actual lender you taking the mortgage out with. By cutting out the middle man, you will probably be able to shave a few days off getting your mortgage offer but this is quite risky. Also if you hold a current account with the lender then you may not need to provide bank statements (this does depend on the bank).

You may get a better interest rate - If you have been banking with a certain lender for a number of years you may be able to secure a lower interest rate, although beware a broker may be able to beat that rate with another lender. Some lenders also do what is called 'dual pricing' this basically when a lender will offer the same client a better interest rate going direct and higher interest rate when going through a broker. The banks argue that since they may be paying the broker a fee for arranging the mortgage it works out cheaper for them for them to offer a slightly lower interest rate when a customer goes direct.

You may feel more comfortable and confident - A bank or any company's reputation can mean a lot to a lot of people, and if you have been banking with a certain bank or have friends or family who have taken out mortgages with a certain lender then you may not feel comfortable applying for a mortgage with a lender you have never heard off; after all, the lender you choose could be the difference between completion or being gazumped.

Now let's move onto the disadvantages of going direct to a bank:

They can only offer what they can offer - This may be a bit of a straight forward one, but when speaking to a bank they will only be able to offer the products they have and they will not be able to advice of better deals or better suited products offered by competitors.

You may have to go into branch - This one is especially true for first time investors, often banks prefer you speak to them face to face which I understand is a service which some people prefer, but for others they will mean time taken off work and you may need to visit the branch on several occasions.

Time - If you are looking for the best rate on the market and maybe you have slightly non-standard criteria, then you will need to spend a lot of time researching and speaking to different lenders. Whereas as when you speak to a broker they will be able search the market and come back to you with a recommendation that fits your needs. One mistake I have seen a lot of people make is applying for the cheapest mortgage on the market with little or no research into the lenders application time to offer. When you speak to a lender direct you not know how many cases they are dealing with at the moment and how long it will take to get your mortgage offer. The lender may say something like "we are taking 15 days on average to produce an offer", although they may be true in some cases, the bit that some lenders will miss out is that this applies to fully packages cases, so cases where the lender has all of the documents they need and all of the those documents are satisfactory, often delays are caused because the documents you provide to a lender are not acceptable and valuation delays can massively slow down the process.

You are just a number on a computer screen - Although this may be the same when speaking to a broker, often when dealing with especially larger lending institutions you will not be assigned a specific contact and if things do go wrong or if you have any questions or may have to spend some time on hold in order to speak to someone qualified who can answer your questions.

The benefits of using a mortgage broker

Time - I think the biggest advantage of using a mortgage broker is that you will save time; nowadays we all live very busy lives and a lot of us would rather spend our spare time doing other things rather than researching the mortgage market. A good broker is worth their weight in gold as they can take out a lot of the hard work of obtaining a mortgage and allow you to spend time with oyu family/friends and enjoying yourself.

Products - A mortgage broker will have access to a lot more mortgage products than your average comparison website and often they can beat any exclusive products that your bank may have offered you.

Contacts within lenders - The mortgage industry is based on people, from people who are taking the mortgage out, to the underwriters at the lenders who are approving them. A decent mortgage broker will have many contacts within numerous lenders so if things do go wrong you will not have to spend hours on the phone trying to find out what happened and a broker may be able to call a certain contact and get issues resolved quickly.

The lifetime of your mortgage - Most people who take a mortgage will have one for potentially decades and during this time you may want to adjust our mortgage or discuss options. If you have started a relationship with a good broker, then often they will be more than happy to take calls whereas when you speak to a bank direct, it is uncertain who you will be talking too. Also, when you come to remortgage, often brokers will set a date in their diary for 3-4 months before your current deal comes to an end so they will remind you that now is the best time to review your mortgage and secure you the next best rate on the market.

There are a few bad things with brokers to consider

Fees - A lot of brokers do charge a fee to use their service, often this fee is recuperated in the mortgage deal your broker finds, but often it is not. I am aware of some brokers who change their fees throughout the year, often in the summer months when the mortgage industry is very busy they will increase their fees and in the winter months things calm down they will reduce their fees. If you want to be super savvy, wait until December time, most brokers in the UK will more than happy to help so you may be able to negotiate a lower broker fee.

Will not have access to every lender - Brokers will have access to numerous deals, but they will not have access to every lender. Some lenders (such as First Direct) do not work with brokers. So it may be best to have a quick look online before speaking to a broker.

It may take longer - By using a mortgage broker you are using a middle man, so if you would like an update on your mortgage, you will need to call the broker who will then need to call the lender who will then need to call you back and potentially ask for further information and then call the lender back and then call you back (you get the idea).

Your Eligibility and Mortgage Criteria

In this section we will look at the key criteria mortgage lenders assess and how your personal circumstances may impact you obtaining a mortgage.

At the time of writing the following criteria is correct, but please bear in mind that things can quickly change and always speak to a broker or lender prior to making any application.

Own your own home

One key piece of buy to let mortgage criteria is to own and live in a residential property (with a mortgage or without) also known as an 'owner occupier'. The reason for this is because mortgage lenders want landlords to have mortgage experience. If you have purchased a residential property with no mortgage or you have inherited a property (and do not own any buy to lets) then you may struggle to get a buy to let. This is where a great broker can come into play and advise you on the best options available for you.

Lender	Do you need to own a residential property upon application?	Quirks
Accord / Yorkshire	Yes	N/A
Aldermore	No	First time landlords needs to be 'owner occupier'
Bank of Ireland / Post Office	Yes	One applicant needs to own a residential property
Barclays	Yes	One applicant needs to own a residential property
Birmingham Midshires / BM Solutions	No	You need to own a property on application (this can be a buy to let)
Clydesdale Bank	Yes	You need to own a property on application (this can be a buy to let)
Godiva (Coventry Building Society)	No	You need to have a residential property at some point
HSBC	No	You need to own a property on application (this can be a buy to let)
Leeds	Yes	One applicant needs to own a residential property
Metro Bank	Yes	N/A
The Mortgage Works	No	You need to own a property on application (this can be a buy to let)
NatWest	No	*NatWest can accept buy to let applications from first time buyers subject to affordability
Newcastle Building	No	You need to own a

Society		property on application (this can be a buy to let)

Nottingham Building Society	Yes	N/A
Principality Building Society	No	You need to have owned a residential property with a mortgage in the previous six months
Santander	Yes	One applicant needs to own a residential property
Skipton	No	You need to have owned a residential property in the previous six months
TSB	No	You need to have owned a property at some point
Virgin Money	Yes	N/A

First time landlords

Another key piece of criteria for mortgage customers is if you have experience as a landlord, typically certain lenders will require you to have at least six months experience of owning and letting out a property with a buy to let mortgage. This can often be a 'catch 22' when some people are unable to obtain buy to let mortgages due to never having a buy to let mortgage in the past.

Please see the below chart for some up to date criteria but always speak to a professional prior to any application.

Lender	Will they lend to first time landlords?	Quirks
Accord / Yorkshire	£25,000	You will need at least 12 months experience as a landlord
Aldermore	Yes	Maximum mortgage of £600,000
Bank of Ireland / Post Office	Yes	N/A
Barclays	Yes	N/A
Birmingham Midshires / BM Solutions	Yes	N/A
Clydesdale Bank	Yes	N/A
Godiva (Coventry Building Society)	Yes	N/A
HSBC	Yes	N/A
Leeds	Yes	N/A
Metro Bank	Yes	N/A
The Mortgage Works	Yes	N/A

| NatWest | Yes | N/A |

Newcastle Building Society	Yes	N/A
Nottingham Building Society	Yes	N/A
Principality Building Society	Yes	N/A
Santander	Yes	N/A
Skipton	Yes	Will only lend for a family/single let
TSB	Yes	N/A
Virgin Money	Yes	N/A

Minimum income requirement

Unlike residential mortgages, buy to let lenders often require their clients to have a minimum income (typically over £25,000). The reason for this is because lenders like their customers to have a separate source of income that can be used to cover a few months of mortgage payments or repairs to the property. Normally the £25,000 is required to be basic salary from employment, so if, for example you have a basic salary £20,000 but receive bonuses that equate to an overall annual income of £25,000 or more then this scenario will not be acceptable by some lenders. If you are self-employed as a sole trader then your net profit is taken into account or if you are a director of a limited company, salary plus any dividends are required to be over £25,000. It is also worth mentioning that rental income is not taken into account when assessing this criteria and the £25,000 needs to be completely separate from buy to let or rental income.

Lender	Minimum income required	Quirks
Accord / Yorkshire	£25,000	N/A
Aldermore	£1,000	First time landlords will need an income of at least £25,000
Bank of Ireland / Post Office	£25,000	N/A
Barclays	£25,000	N/A
Birmingham Midshires / BM Solutions	£1	You must have at least one source of income non property related
Clydesdale Bank	£30,000	Your income will need to be at least £75,000 if you own more than four buy to lets
Godiva (Coventry Building Society)	£25,000	N/A
HSBC	£25,000	N/A
Leeds	£25,000	£40,000 for holiday lets
Metro Bank	£1	You must have at least one source of income non property related
The Mortgage Works	£1	N/A

NatWest	£25,000	N/A
Newcastle Building Society	£25,000	N/A
Nottingham Building Society	£30,000	N/A
Principality Building Society	£20,000	N/A
Santander	£25,000	N/A
Skipton	£20,000	N/A
TSB	£25,000	N/A
Virgin Money	£25,000	N/A

Your Age

Your age may have a very big impact when it comes to determining how long you have your buy to let mortgage for. Unlike residential mortgages, a lot of buy to let lending is non-regulated meaning the lenders can be more relaxed when it comes to lending into retirement and the length of mortgage you can have. Often lenders will take a common sense approach to the term of your mortgage as this is an investment and will produce an income so if you pass away, become ill or lose your job etc. there will be a tenant who will be able to cover their mortgage repayments. Most residential mortgage lenders require their applicants to be age 18 as a minimum but with buy to let this can vary from ages 21 to 25. On the other end of the scale most lenders have a maximum age of 75 but there is a few who have no maximum age whatsoever but often a maximum age at application, so in theory a 70 year old could take out a 35 year mortgage until age 105!

This in an area of buy to let lending which may become more relaxed over the coming years due to pension freedoms and a lot of people withdrawing lump sums from their pensions to invest in property.

Lender	Minimum age	Maximum age at end of term	Maximum age upon application
Accord / Yorkshire	25	75	70
Aldermore	25 for first time landlords or 21 for experienced landlords	85	78
Bank of Ireland / Post Office	21	80	74
Barclays	21	80	74
Birmingham Midshires / BM Solutions	25	80	74
Clydesdale Bank	18	75	69
Godiva (Coventry Building Society)	18	85	75
HSBC	18	No max	N/A
Leeds	18	80	74
Metro Bank	21	80	74

The Mortgage Works	21	No Max	70
NatWest	18	70	66
Newcastle Building Society	21	No max	N/A
Nottingham Building Society	25	75	72
Principality Building Society	21	76	70
Santander	21	75	69
Skipton	18	85	79
TSB	25	75	69
Virgin Money	21	76	68

Maximum Portfolio Size

If you are an experienced landlord who has built up a portfolio it is important to consider a lot of lenders will try to limit the amount of properties you can own. I believe this is due to risk, as often lenders do not want to lend too much to a single borrower for risk of default or sudden changes in the market. Often mortgage lenders will also count unencumbered (mortgage free) properties towards the maximum and also your main residence. Typically what we find is the more 'high street' lenders have stricter portfolio rules whereas lenders who have been in the market for a long time or are more niche (who may charge higher rates) can be more relaxed. Due to recent PRA regulation, if you have more than 4 buy to let properties lenders will need to conduct more thorough checks and look at your portfolio as a whole so the next time you speak with your broker it is worth having the mortgage balances, property values, monthly mortgage repayments and rental income figures handy.

Lender	Minimum portfolio	Quirks
Accord / Yorkshire	15 properties	10 can be mortgaged
Aldermore	10 properties	10 Aldermore, unlimited elsewhere
Bank of Ireland / Post Office	3 properties	N/A
Barclays	6 properties or £4.5m	N/A
Birmingham Midshires / BM Solutions	None	Three within the Lloyds Banking group, so BM Solutions, Halifax, Scottish Widows etc.
Clydesdale Bank	8 properties	3 properties or £1m of lending with Clydesdale, your income will also need to be higher than your annual rental income
Godiva (Coventry Building Society)	10 properties	3 properties or £1m of lending with Godiva
HSBC	5 properties with HSBC	5 properties with HSBC or £2m across all lenders
Leeds	8 properties	Includes unencumbered
Metro Bank	15 properties	Includes unencumbered, max 10 with Metro

The Mortgage Works	None	N/A
NatWest	4 mortgaged properties	Unencumbered and residential are not included
Newcastle Building Society	3	Does not include unencumbered
Nottingham Building Society	None	Maximum of 10 properties with Nottingham, total of £1.5m
Principality Building Society	5 properties	Includes unencumbered buy to lets but not residential
Santander	7 properties	7 properties including unencumbered, maximum 5 with Santander
Skipton	10 properties	Maximum 5 with Skipton or £1.5m with Skipton
TSB	11 properties	N/A
Virgin Money	11 properties	Maximum 4 with Virgin or £2m with Virgin

First Time Buyer Buy to Let

So you want to buy a buy to let property as a first time buyer? As you will probably be aware residential mortgages require at least a 5% deposit but as mentioned with a buy to let mortgages you will need at least 25%. So if you are purchasing a property valued at £100,000, you need to put down at least £25,000. You may have heard of some buy to let lenders allowing a deposit as little as 15%-20% but unfortunately because you are a first time buyer you will need at least 25%.

Most buy to let lenders will base the amount you borrow on the rental income for the property. So for example if you are going to receive £500/m in rent then typically a lender will use the £500 and work out the amount you can borrow. As someone seeking a first time buyer buy to let mortgage, the lender will also look at the affordability for your mortgage. So very similar to a standard residential mortgage, the lender will carry out an affordability assessment looking at your income and outgoings and the mortgage will have to 'fit' on both assessments. It is also worth mentioning that you will need to have an income of at least £25,000 (not including any rent you may receive).

The only high street at the moment who will be willing to offer a first time buyer buy to let mortgage is NatWest but are some more niche lenders (usually with higher interests) who can lend in this area.

Limited Company Buy to Lets

We will discuss the benefits of buying/owning property through a limited company later, however when it comes to obtaining finance you will be limited with mortgage options. At the moment it is only specialist lenders who lend in this area although this may change in the coming years as this strategy becomes more common place. Some of the below lenders only lend through brokers so you may need to speak to a mortgage broker in order to arrange this type of mortgage. A lot of the below lenders have specific deals for limited company buy to lets but often require less rental income due to less tax being paid.

Lender	Quirks
Aldermore	N/A
Axis Bank	Will only lend to SPVs, minimum of 4 directors for the business
Fleet	N/A
Foundation Home Loans	Will only lend to SPVs, minimum of 4 directors for the business
Kent Reliance	Will only lend to SPVs, minimum of 4 directors for the business
Keystone	N/A
Market Harborough	Only for commercial properties
National Counties	Maximum LTV 65%, minimum loan size of £75,000
Paragon	At least 80% of shares need to be owned by the director/s
Precise Mortgages	N/A
Shawbrook Bank	Can potentially be trading in another unrelated business
Vida Homeloans	N/A

Minimum Time in UK

If you have recently moved to the UK, or if you have spent a prolonged period of time out of the UK, (usually over 6 months) then you may struggle to obtain a buy to let mortgage. The reason for this is down to credit scoring, if you have lived in another country you may not have maintained a credit history while you have been away. This section is for applications that have permanent rights to reside in the UK, we will discuss your options if you currently hold a visa in the next segment.

Lender	Minimum time in the UK
Accord / Yorkshire	3 years
Aldermore	2 years
Bank of Ireland / Post Office	3 years
Barclays	2 years
Birmingham Midshires / BM Solutions	12 months
Clydesdale Bank	2 years
Godiva (Coventry Building Society)	1 month
HSBC	1 month
Leeds	2 years
Metro Bank	3 years
The Mortgage Works	3 years
NatWest	6 months
Newcastle Building Society	3 years
Nottingham Building Society	2 years
Principality Building Society	2 years
Santander	1 month
Skipton	12 months
TSB	12 months
Virgin Money	3 years

Visa Criteria

This section is in regard to applicants who are permanently living in the UK and are currently on a visa. The majority of mortgage lenders will need you have permanent rights to reside but some lenders can be a lot more flexible, however you will often need to earn a certain level of income or may need to put down a higher deposit than usual. The length of time you have on your visa and the type of visa you have can also impact your lending options so it is very important to speak to a good broker as they will be provide expert advice tailored to your specific needs.

Lender	Does the lender need permanent rights to reside	Quirks
Accord / Yorkshire	Yes	N/A
Aldermore	Yes	N/A
Bank of Ireland / Post Office	Yes	N/A
Barclays	Yes	N/A
Birmingham Midshires / BM Solutions	No	Must have 3 years remaining in visa
Clydesdale Bank	No	You will need to earn at least £75,000, you will need to put down a 30% deposit, tier one/tier two visas only and you will need at least 12 months remaining on visa
Godiva (Coventry Building Society)	Yes	N/A
HSBC	No	You will need an income of at least £75,000
Leeds	Yes	N/A
Metro Bank	Yes	N/A
The Mortgage Works	Yes	N/A
NatWest	Yes	N/A

Newcastle Building Society	Yes	N/A
Nottingham Building Society	Yes	N/A
Principality Building Society	No	You will need at least 2 years remaining on visa
Santander	Yes	N/A
Skipton	Yes	N/A
TSB	Yes	N/A
Virgin Money	Yes	N/A

Maximum Number of Applicants

A very good strategy for building your portfolio quicker is to pool resources with family/fiends/business partners in order to purchase a property. This can be a very good option because the initial outlay can be shared between up to four individuals and this can also minimise risk as this is shared out. If this is a strategy you are looking into then it is very important to have a business plan and a clear exit strategy as this can solve a lot of problems later down the line. When it comes to obtaining a mortgage there is a large portion of lenders who can consider up to four applicants on an application and to minimise the paper work you can only use one applicant's income to meet the lenders minimum income requirements. Due to the nature of this type of application it can often take longer to obtain a mortgage offer as more underwriting will be needed on the case and some lenders will require you to complete a paper application form instead of submitting an application online.

Lender	Maximum number of applicants	Quirks
Accord / Yorkshire	2	N/A
Aldermore	2	N/A
Bank of Ireland / Post Office	4	N/A
Barclays	4	N/A
Birmingham Midshires / BM Solutions	4	N/A
Clydesdale Bank	4	N/A
Godiva (Coventry Building Society)	4	N/A
HSBC	2	N/A
Leeds	4	N/A
Metro Bank	4	Must be family members
The Mortgage Works	2	N/A
NatWest	2	N/A
Newcastle Building Society	2	N/A
Nottingham Building Society	4	N/A
Principality Building Society	4	N/A
Santander	2	N/A
Skipton	4	Paper application if more than 2 applicants
TSB	4	N/A

| Virgin Money | 4 | N/A |

Let to Buy

As we already discussed, let to buy can be a great strategy in order to build your portfolio and in this section we will discuss the buy to let remortgage element. So just to re-cap, a let to buy is when you let out your existing residential property while simultaneously purchasing a new residential property for yourself to live in. The most important element of this type of transaction is the buy to let remortgage side, the majority of lenders will need you to have an offer accepted on your new residential home and will require you to complete both mortgages on the same day.

One very frustrating pitfall can occur when it comes to the underwriting of your mortgages. All mortgage lenders will assess documents (such as payslips/bank statements etc.) before they issue the formal mortgage offer. Certain lenders will have a requirement to see the mortgage offer from the other lender before they will issue their formal mortgage offer. So if you chose the wrong mortgage lenders, this can sometimes cause a stalemate as each lender will not issue their offer until the other lender does.

Lender	Does the lender allow you to remortgage your existing home into a buy to let in order to purchase a new residential property	Quirks
Accord / Yorkshire	Yes	You will need to be an experienced landlord (so have at least 12 months of letting experience with another buy to let), also they will need to see the formal mortgage offer for your new residential property
Aldermore	Yes	Aldermen will need to see a copy of the residential mortgage offer prior to completion
Bank of Ireland / Post Office	Yes	Will need simultaneous completion
Barclays	Yes	N/A
Birmingham Midshires / BM Solutions	Yes	Specific mortgage products
Clydesdale Bank	Yes	Does not need an offer accepted on the new property but they will do affordability checks
Godiva (Coventry Building Society)	No	N/A
HSBC	No	N/A

Leeds	Yes	Specific mortgage products

Metro Bank	Yes	You will need to own at least one other buy to let property
The Mortgage Works	Yes	Will need to see residential mortgage offer and will need same solicitor for the buy to let remortgage and onward purchase
NatWest	Yes	If you are raising capital for a deposit then your NatWest mortgage will need to have a lower loan to value in comparison to your new residential mortgage
Newcastle Building Society	Yes	N/A
Nottingham Building Society	Yes	Will need simultaneous completion

Principality Building Society	Yes	N/A
Santander	No	N/A
Skipton	Yes	N/A
TSB	Yes	N/A
Virgin Money	Yes	N/A

Sole Owner Joint Proprietor

'Sole owner joint proprietor' can be a great way to avoid the additional 3% stamp duty charge on a second property. Sole owner joint proprietor is essentially having one person named on the deeds of the property and two or more people named on the mortgage. This option can avoid the additional stamp duty due to technically only one person (usually a non-property owning person) having their name named on the deeds.

At the moment there is one big lender who can consider this type of transaction and this is Barclays, another one is Metro Bank. It is important to remember that you will need to meet all of the lenders other criteria and it is important to get tax advice to see if this option will be the best for you.

Raising Capital without an Offer Accepted On a Buy to Let

When it comes to expanding your portfolio a great option can be to release additional capital from a property when you remortgage in order to put this towards a deposit for a new buy to let purchase.

As buy to let is seem more as a business then lenders can be a lot more relaxed when it comes to requiring evidence of the specific property you are looking to purchase. However some lenders will require the details of the specific property before they are able to release funds. Some lenders may only require rough details in regard to purchase price, estimated rental income and location, whereas others will need evidence of a specific property. If you have not found a property yet it is possible for the funds to be released however it is important to consider you will pay interest on the additional borrowing.

Lender	Can you raise capital through a remortgage for a new buy to let purchase?	Quirks
Accord / Yorkshire	Yes	Will ask for further information such a monthly payment and size of other mortgage
Aldermore	Yes	Will not need details for new buy to let property
Bank of Ireland / Post Office	Yes	Will need new property address
Barclays	Yes	Will need details of new property
Birmingham Midshires / BM Solutions	Yes	Will not need details for new buy to let property
Clydesdale Bank	Yes	Will ask for further information such a monthly payment and size of other mortgage
Godiva (Coventry Building Society)	Yes	Will not need details for new buy to let property
HSBC	Yes	Will need details of new buy to let property
Leeds	Yes	Will not need details for new buy to let property
Metro Bank	Yes	Will need details of new buy to let property

The Mortgage Works	Yes	Will not need details for new buy to let property
NatWest	Yes	Will need details of new buy to let property
Newcastle Building Society	Yes	Will need details of new buy to let property
Nottingham Building Society	Yes	Will not need details for new buy to let property
Principality Building Society	Yes	Will not need details for new buy to let property
Santander	Yes	Will ask for further information such a monthly payment and size of other mortgage
Skipton	Yes	Will not need details for new buy to let property
TSB	Yes	Will not need details for new buy to let property
Virgin Money	Yes	Will not need details for new buy to let property

Minimum Loan Size / Minimum Property Value

If you are looking to potentially purchase a cheaper property then you need to be aware most lenders do have minimum loan sizes/property values. The reason for this is because the administration costs for setting up a new mortgage can cost a few hundred pounds and often mortgages can be the cheapest way of borrowing in comparison to personal loans/credit cards etc. so lenders often do not want to devote resources to setting up, valuing properties, paying for legal work etc. for a loan which will not produce a good return.

The reason I have decided to cover both minimum loan size and minimum property value together is because some lenders have no minimum loan size however they have a minimum property value. When we combine both of these elements together it means it can be difficult (or almost impossible) to obtain a mortgage on a property valued at less than £40,000 (so minimum loan size of £30,000).

Lender	Minimum loan size	Minimum property value
Accord / Yorkshire	£50,000	£75,000
Aldermore	£25,000	£60,000
Bank of Ireland / Post Office	£25,001	£60,000
Barclays	£35,000	£58,333
Birmingham Midshires / BM Solutions	£25,001	£40,000
Clydesdale Bank	£80,000	£0
Godiva (Coventry Building Society)	£25,001	£75,000
HSBC	£25,000	£0
Leeds	£0 (£75,000 for a holiday let)	£50,000 (£70,000 for properties in south east England and £85,000 for properties in London)
Metro Bank	£50,000	£100,000
The Mortgage Works	£25,001	£50,000
NatWest	£25,000	£50,000
Newcastle Building Society	£25,000	£75,000
Nottingham Building Society	£30,000	£70,000
Principality Building Society	£25,001	£50,000 (£75,000 in London)
Santander	£25,000	£75,000
Skipton	£5,000	£50,000

TSB	£25,005	£50,000
Virgin Money	£0	£50,000

Minimum/Maximum Term (Length of Mortgage)

As previously discussed the length if your mortgage will be determined by your age, if you are taking your mortgage out on an interest only basis, then the actual length of the mortgage will not affect your monthly repayments as you are only paying interest. So you could have a 5 year mortgage or a 25 year mortgage and you will pay exactly the same each month, so I would always advise to try and take the mortgage for as long as possible (if on interest only). If your mortgage is on a repayment basis then it is important to consider what your monthly repayments will be and if the property was not let out could you afford to keep up with payments. Different to standard residential mortgages a lot of lenders for buy to let often have a minimum term of 5 years and a maximum term of 25 years.

Lender	Minimum term of mortgage	Maximum term of mortgage
Accord / Yorkshire	5 years	35 years
Aldermore	6 years	35 years
Bank of Ireland / Post Office	5 years	35 years
Barclays	5 years	25 years
Birmingham Midshires / BM Solutions	5 years	40 years
Clydesdale Bank	5 years	25 years
Godiva (Coventry Building Society)	1 year	35 years
HSBC	5 years	25 years
Leeds	5 years	40 years
Metro Bank	5 years	35 years
The Mortgage Works	5 years	35 years
NatWest	3 years	35 years
Newcastle Building Society	5 years	25 years
Nottingham Building Society	3 years	25 years
Principality Building Society	5 years	40 years
Santander	5 years	25 years
Skipton	5 years	35 years (25 years for interest only)
TSB	5 years	40 years
Virgin Money	7 years	25 years

Can Arrangement Fees Be Added Above Loan to Values

As previously discussed in this book, buy to let mortgages tend to attract higher arrangement fees in comparison to standard residential mortgages. Most lenders will allow you to add these to the mortgage, however if by adding the fee if it takes the mortgage balance above a loan to value bracket then you may have to pay this fee upfront or slightly reduce the amount you are looking to borrow. I would always advice to borrow slightly less and increase your deposit as often these are non-refundable or can take a while to get back if the mortgage does not proceed. You should know by now the amount you can borrow on a buy to let mortgage is dictated by the amount of rental income you will receive (amongst other things) so if you are adding an arrangement fee to the mortgage balance then your rental income will need to be sufficient to meet the new total borrowing.

Lender	Can an arrangement fee be added above the loan to value bracket?	Can an arrangement fee be added above the minimum rental income required?
Accord / Yorkshire	Yes	No
Aldermore	Yes	No
Bank of Ireland / Post Office	Yes	Yes
Barclays	Yes	No
Birmingham Midshires / BM Solutions	Yes	Yes
Clydesdale Bank	Yes	Yes
Godiva (Coventry Building Society)	Yes	No
HSBC	No	No
Leeds	Yes	No
Metro Bank	Yes	Yes
The Mortgage Works	Yes	Yes
NatWest	Yes	Yes
Newcastle Building Society	No	No
Nottingham Building Society	No	Yes
Principality Building Society	Yes	No
Santander	Yes	Yes
Skipton	Yes	Yes
TSB	Yes	No
Virgin Money	Yes	Yes

How Long Are Mortgage Offers Valid For?

When you come to purchase a property it is important to find out or have a good indication of when you are looking to complete on the purchase. A typical mortgage offer is valid for usually between 3– 6 months and under the right circumstances it can sometimes be extended (usually on a case by case basis and can dependent of when the valuation was carried out and dependent on the lender). If you are buying a property which is in a long chain and there is potential things could be delayed then choosing the correct lender is paramount as you don't want to pay for a valuation, legal work and then be delayed by a few weeks and your mortgage offer expiring. If your mortgage offer does expire then you will usually need to submit a new application with the mortgage lender, it is always worth asking if they can cross-reference any documentation you have already submitted and if they can use the valuation which has already been carried out to save yourself a lot of time/money. When it comes to new build properties, there is always the risk of a delay so most lenders can be more flexible.

Lender	How long is a mortgage offer valid for?	Quirks
Accord / Yorkshire	6 months	N/A
Aldermore	80 days	6 months for new builds
Bank of Ireland / Post Office	6 months	N/A
Barclays	6 months	6 months from application
Birmingham Midshires / BM Solutions	6 months from valuation	Yes
Clydesdale Bank	180 days	Yes
Godiva (Coventry Building Society)	4 months / 6 months	4 months for remortgage cases, 6 months for purchase cases
HSBC	6 months	No
Leeds	6 months	No
Metro Bank	3 months	6 months for new build properties
The Mortgage Works	3 months / 6 months	3 months for remortgage cases / 6 months for purchases and let to buy cases
NatWest	6 months	New build purchase offers can be extended by 1 month
Newcastle Building Society	3 months	N/A
Nottingham Building Society	6 months	N/A
Principality Building Society	3 months	6 months for new builds
Santander	6 months	6 months from valuation
Skipton	6 months	N/A
TSB	Product specific	Each product has a specific deadline, however you can

		change product at a later stage
Virgin Money	16 weeks	N/A

Studio Flats

Buying smaller flats as buy to let investments can be a very good strategy as these properties are a lot easier to maintain and depending on location you could secure a professional tenant who will look after the property. This type of investment can however have a larger turnover of tenants as naturally people get older, secure a better job and may want to move somewhere bigger with a partner or to start a family. When it comes to obtaining finance you can be limited with options and as a general rule it is best to have a minimum floor space of 30 square meters. A mortgage lender may allow studio flats in their published criteria; however the property will be subject to 'valuer's comments' meaning they could decline the application based on the property. 'Valuers comments' is a term used to describe when a mortgage lender arranges a survey to be carried out and the surveyor will make an informed decision if the property is adequate security once they have physically been to and valued the property. So it is almost impossible to be 100% certain if a lender will be happy to lend but it is important to check the property fits criteria prior to any application.

Lender	Will they lend on a studio flat?	Quirks
Accord / Yorkshire	No	N/A
Aldermore	No	N/A
Bank of Ireland / Post Office	No	N/A
Barclays	No	N/A
Birmingham Midshires / BM Solutions	Yes	No minimum square footage, however it will be subject to valuer's comments
Clydesdale Bank	Yes	Minimum 30 sqm
Godiva (Coventry Building Society)	No	N/A
HSBC	Yes	Minimum 30 sqm
Leeds	No	N/A
Metro Bank	No	N/A
The Mortgage Works	Yes	Minimum 30 sqm
NatWest	Yes	Minimum 30 sqm
Newcastle Building Society	No	N/A
Nottingham Building Society	No	N/A
Principality Building Society	No	N/A
Santander	Yes	No minimum square footage
Skipton	No	N/A
TSB	Yes	No minimum square footage
Virgin Money	No	N/A

How Many Years Need To Be Left On The Lease?

When it comes to purchasing a leasehold property, probably the most important question to ask is how many years are left on the lease? At the end of the lease period (often over one hundred years) the property will return to the freeholder so lenders are not very keen if a property has a low number of years left. The majority of leasehold properties are flats although it is not uncommon for some house to also be leasehold. A lease is essentially in place to provide neighbouring houses/flats with rules in regard to repairs and to maintain communal areas. I would personally advice to ideally have at least 85 years left on a lease as anything lower can cause issues and the lower the number of years on the lease the more expensive it can be to get it extended. If you own a property, or if you are looking to purchase a property with a low number of years left on the lease then similar to studio flats it will be subject to 'valuer's comments' so a lender's criteria may state they will lend however it will be down to the surveyor who values the property.

It is not only the number of years left on a lease you need to consider, you also need to think about how long you would like your mortgage term. Most lenders will require a certain number of years left on the lease combined with the length of your mortgage, for example a lender may require 40 years at the end of the term, so if you are looking to take out a 25 year mortgage then the lease will need to have 65 years remaining (40 + 25 = 65).

A common issue some borrowers face is if they are looking to remortgage a property and borrow additional funds to extend a lease and at the time of application they will not meet the lenders criteria. Some lenders can be quite flexible in this scenario and there is a niche lender who can consider applications with no lease in place at the time of application, subject to one being in place at completion.

Lender	Minimum years left on a lease	Number of years required at the end of the mortgage term
Accord / Yorkshire	85	50
Aldermore	60 (can consider applications with no lease in place but a lease will need to be in place at completion)	40
Bank of Ireland / Post Office	80	50
Barclays	25 years + mortgage term	25 years + mortgage term
Birmingham Midshires / BM Solutions	70	30
Clydesdale Bank	50	25
Godiva (Coventry Building Society)	70	35
HSBC	40	35
Leeds	85	45
Metro Bank	55	50
The Mortgage Works	70	30
NatWest	38	35
Newcastle Building Society	85	Will always need 85 years
Nottingham Building Society	85	60
Principality Building Society	85	45
Santander	55 (Will ideally want 99 years)	30
Skipton	45 (can consider applications with no lease in place but a lease will need to be in	40

| | place at completion) | |

TSB	70	30
Virgin Money	70	45

HMOs

We have discussed HMOs on several occasions throughout the book and I have mentioned it can be difficult to obtain finance on this type of investment. Due to the time and commitment that needs to be put in it is advisable to gain some experience letting out another type of investment prior to tackling a HMO. Most mortgage lenders who lend in this area also feel the same way as often you will need at least three years of letting experience and may need to own several other buy to lets before you will be eligible.

Before you embark on a HMO investment it is important to realise the additional costs when it comes this type of property. The overall wear and tear will be higher due to the nature of tenants moving in and out and having a larger number of people in the property. Another cost is

HMO licensing, depending on the local authority you may need to pay for a license to make sure the property is safe. Out of the limited lenders you will have access to you will usually have to pay a higher rate of interest and there are often additional fees payable.

When it comes to defining a HMO, mortgage lenders often have their own definitions but the standard description is at least three separate unrelated individuals renting on separate tenancy agreements. Most lenders will need at least one living room and kitchen.

Lender	Criteria
Aldermore	You will need at least 3 years of letting experience and Aldermore have a maximum number of bedrooms as 6
Axis Bank	You will need at least 2 years of letting experience, you will need to own at least 3 buy to let properties at time of application and maximum of 6 bedrooms
Fleet	You will need at least 3 years of letting experience
Kent Reliance	They can consider applications up to 85% loan to value and can consider up to 8 bedrooms
Keystone	Maximum of 6 bedrooms
Leeds	You will need a minimum 12 months letting experience, up to a maximum of 5 bedrooms, when remortgaging you will not be eligible for free legal work
The Mortgage Works	You will need a minimum of 6 months letting experience, maximum 7 bedrooms, maximum loan to value of 65%

Paragon	You will need a minimum of 3 years letting experience, minimum valuation of property £100,000
Precise Mortgages	You will need to own at least 2 buy to lets for at least 2 years, minimum valuation in London is £250,000, elsewhere is £150,000, up to 6 bedrooms

How Tenant Types Can Affect Mortgages

Family Let / Professional Lets

When it comes to mortgage lenders, the ideal investment they are looking to finance is a family/professional let. As discussed previously, this type of tenant will often pay their rent on time and look after the property. Mortgage lenders will always look at the worst case scenario, which would be if they had to repossess the property and how quickly they could sell the property in order to regain their money. Often there is a large market for family homes so lenders can often easily sell this type of property easily and quickly. Also due to the nature of this type of investment being the less risky there is less chance of tenant not paying their rent or destroying the property which dramatically increases the likely of the borrower paying their mortgage payments.

Student Lets / Larger Professional Lets On a Single AST

Until recently it used to be a lot harder to obtain finance for this type of tenant, however if you can manage to have the tenants (usually a group of friends) sign one single assured shorthold tenancy agreement you will open up a lot more options. Most lenders will have a maximum number of tenants on one tenancy agreement (usually 4 or 5) as this will make the overall investment a lot easier to manage as a whole. Also, if the mortgage lender needs to repossess the property there is just one agreement in place which will end at the same time, thus making eviction easier at the end of the tenancy. It is very important to bear in mind that when a lender values the rental income for this type property they will assess the property as if it was let to a family (not let on an individual room basis) and most lenders will need there to be a living room, as often some landlords will convert a downstairs living room/dining room into an additional bedroom.

DSS

Letting a property to an individual or family who is in receipt of housing benefit can cause some issues with some lenders. Although this is not always the case and often unfairly, this type of tenant may not pay their rent on time or if the property has to be repossessed there is a chance they may cause damage to the lenders security. These typically lower priced properties may be harder to sell so some lenders often stay clear. An important factor when obtaining a mortgage is if the tenant will pay their rent direct to the landlord or if the landlord will receive this direct the local council.

HMOs / Student Lets With Multiple Tenancy Agreements

There has been a lot of press and a lot of 'hype' around HMOs as the yield can be a lot higher than the average returns on a family let for example. Almost all high street lenders do not lend on this type of this property due to the amount of time and commitment it takes to manage one. The last thing a lender wants if they repossess a property is to take the time and money to manage this type of investment until the final tenant finishes their agreement.

Remotgaging

We have discussed a lot about taking a mortgage out to purchase a property but what about when you come to remortgage? Remortgaging is an important part when it comes to building your portfolio and securing the best possible returns on your investment if you have a mortgage. After your initial deal has come to an end (for example a 2/3/5 year fix etc.) The best thing to do is remortgage. When you remortgage you essentially move your mortgage to a new mortgage lender and they will repay your existing lender and often offer you a better interest rate in comparison to the standard variable rate (SVR) your existing lender will charge. In an ideal world you will never have the pay your existing lenders higher rate. Most mortgage offers are valid for 3-6 months and will take around 6-8 weeks to obtain a mortgage offer and also complete the necessary legal work. I would advise to look into remortgaging around three months before your existing deal comes to an end and ideally have your new mortgage begin the day after your current deal ends. It is estimated that over four million households are currently paying the SVR and this can be easily changed by phoning your existing lender or speaking to a broker.

Releasing Equity

One very important factor when you come to remortgage is if you would like to release any equity. If your property has gained value since you bought it or last remortgaged then you may be able to borrow against this. Depending on your strategy, a lot of landlords will borrow more money above their mortgage balance when they remortgage in order to put this towards a deposit on a new property. As we have previously discussed the amount you can borrow for a buy to let mortgage is largely based on the rental income you receive each month. As of 2017 the PRA has introduced new regulations which can make it harder to release equity so it is best to get the correct professional advice to see if and how much you will be able to release. If you are looking to release equity to purchase a new buy to let then often mortgage lenders will not need an offer accepted a new place as long as you can provide an area, type of property, type of tenant and estimated rental income you expect to receive.

Loan to Values

Your loan to value (LTV) is the ratio between the value of your property and your mortgage balance. For example, if you own a property valued at £100,000 and you have an outstanding mortgage of £70,000 you will have a loan to value of 70%. When you come to remortgage it is important to look closely at your LTV as sometimes you may have an outstanding balance which is slightly above a threshold, for example you may have a balance of £71,000 on a property valued at £100,000 where you can make an overpayment of £1,000 in order to reach the 70% LTV which could result in a better rate of interest.

Chapter 3

Management of your investment

How to Find Tenants

Your tenant/s will ultimately make or break your investment so it is very important you find a reliable person to let your property too. We have all seen television shows with nightmare tenants who don't pay their rent or destroy the property. This does happen, but it is quite rare. You can limit this risk by doing thorough research before handing over the keys.

If you are looking to find your own tenants, it is well worth the time and money to carry out a thorough background check. The main place to start is to find out a bit about your tenant, so maybe ask what they do for a living, where they have lived previously and why they are moving to the area. A great tip is to ask for three months of bank statements and take a look at their income and expenditure to determine how comfortably they can afford the property. If you see numerous gambling transactions or payday loans this may also give you an indication of how they manage their finances. You can also ask for a reference from a previous landlord or their employer, if they are unwilling to provide this then it may be best to look for someone else. Credit reference agencies can also provide you with a very good indication on how well they manage their finances by looking at their history of paying bills on time.

If all the above seems like too much work (maybe you have a full time job) you can also ask a letting agent to do this for, although there will be a fee.

There are numerous ways to find a tenant for your investment, here a few examples:

Online

Probably the most common way of finding a tenant (or almost anything for that matter) is through the internet. You will have access to numerous potential tenants after advertising online. If you are looking to let your property as soon as possible then you may have to have pay for this service but there a few very good cheaper (sometimes free) alternatives.

OpenRent.co.uk

OpenRent is probably the UK's number one website for finding a tenant, you can advertise for free or you can pay a small fee to rank your advert higher than everyone else's. At the time of writing they will give you a free 5 day advert on RightMove (which is probably the UK's number one property portal).

Spareroom.co.uk

This website is mainly designed for people who would like to rent out a spare room they may have. Although a lot of landlords advertise entire properties on there, due to the service being free.

Gumtree.co.uk

Gumtree is probably the UK's number one website for buying or selling second hand items but it is also an extremely popular website for advertising rental properties. You can use the site for free but be careful as it does have a reputation for sometimes attracting the wrong type of tenant, so please do a thorough background check before letting your property.

There are also numerous other website where you can pay a fee for a company to advertise and manage your viewings. If you are looking to find your own tenant, by using the previously mentioned websites you should be able to advertise to the majority of potentially tenants (for potentially free).

Social Media

A large majority of people use social media on a daily basis and one way of finding a reliable tenant may be to post on your social media account. If you receive a recommendation from a reliable friend or associate, then this can often lead to a reliable tenant and investment. Similar to Gumtree, Facebook now has a marketplace where you can advertise your property as well which is great because you will be able to check out any potential tenants profiles to see what they are like. I would avoid letting a property to a friend as if they are unable to pay the rent this certainly adds another level of complexity to retrieve rent arrears.

Traditional Methods

Advertise in your local newspaper

If you were reading this maybe ten years ago, I would definitely advice to place an Ad in your local newspaper or magazine. Although you will probably get a lot more exposure through the internet, there are still a great number of people who read their local newspaper every day. Probably the best time to advertise would be on the weekend when the majority of people are not at work and read newspapers/magazines.

Advertise in the local area

This option is probably a little outdated, but some people do find long term reliable tenants via this method. Some ideas could be to post paper adverts with the property's details in local shops, parks and any area where people generally congregate. One must (if your potential letting agent isn't doing this already with a sign outside) is to place an advert in the window of the property you are looking to let out (just make sure you include your phone number/email address).

Managing the Tenant Finding Process

If you are looking to find your own tenant or if you are paying an agent to do this for you, it is vitally important that you reply to any communications you may receive as soon as possible and keep notes on what is happening. The market moves quickly and if you take a few days to reply to a potential tenant there is a chance that they have found somewhere else. Also if you are using an agent, it is very important to keep in touch with them to see what is happening and if they are unable to find a suitable tenant within a period of time it is also worth considering using another agent who can (time is money). I am a big fan of setting goals and if you don't find a tenant within a certain timeframe then it may best to change your strategy.

Checks To Carry Out Prior To Letting Your Property

So once you have found a potential tenant it is important to carry out the correct checks prior to agreeing to the tenancy. This is a very important step in the process as making one wrong decision could take up a lot of time and cost you a lot of money. If you are using a letting agent please make sure they have carried out the below checks as it will be your name on the tenancy agreement if things go wrong.

Right to Rent Checks

Until recently this wasn't a requirement of landlords but landlords now have the legal obligation to carry out this check. It is to essentially check if a person has the legal right to rent a property in the UK. Even if a tenant is not named on the tenancy agreement and they are aged over 18 then this check must be carried out. The right to rent check can be carried out by obtaining original documents such as a UK passport, European passport, permanent rights to reside documentation, birth certificate and driving license etc. It is very important you make copies of these documents and keep a record of dates, I would advise to check on the Gov.uk website because this legal obligation and requirement may change or be updated. If you are using a letting agent to rent out your property it is important to ask if they have carried out this check because it will be yourself who has the legal obligation.

Deposit Protection Scheme

If your tenant is paying a deposit before you let out your property then it is very important you place this deposit in a Deposit Protection Scheme. This scheme is designed to protect your tenants deposit at the end of the tenancy. The guidelines state that when you receive the deposit, within thirty days you must place this deposit in an authorised scheme where this money cannot be touched and you must notify your tenant of their rights and the scheme details. The scheme is designed to help tenants obtain their deposit back without any issues if they met all of the conditions of the tenancy, haven't damaged the property and they have paid their rent and bills on time.

The Overall Safety of the Property

The overall safety and any major repairs which may be needed will be your responsibility, as previously discussed when you purchase your property you can opt to have a detailed survey carried out which can provide you with a lot detail in regard to the conditional of the property. Being a landlord means you will be responsible for any major works needed (such as structural repairs, the roof, plumbing, electricals etc.) however your tenant may be responsible for any minor repairs and the general upkeep of the property.

Gas and Electrical Certificates

As a landlord you will also be responsible for the safety of the gas and electricity in the property. Prior to letting out your property it is vitally important you have a qualified professional check the safety of the property and also keep a record this which may need to be provided to your tenant.

Energy Performance Certificate (EPC)

If you are looking to let out or sell a property in the property it is now a legal obligation to provide your potential buyer or tenant with an EPC. An EPC essentially looks at how energy efficient a property is and takes into account insulation, if the property uses gas or electricity among other things. If you are renovating a property it is a perfect opportunity to try and increase this because it may make your property easier to sell or let out.

A Detailed Inventory

The key word in this section is 'detailed'. If you are providing your tenant with any furniture or appliances it is very important to detail everything that will be included with the tenancy. You can even list the items age and conditions and it is important you (or your letting agent) asks both parties to sign and date the inventory which can be used to cover any damage when the tenancy comes to an end.

The Tenancy Agreement

A tenancy agreement is a legal document which is designed to lay out the rights and responsibilities of both the tenant and landlord. If the tenancy agreement is for less than three years then you can legally agree a verbal tenancy, however this is strongly advised against because if things don't work out then it is your word against theirs, if a tenancy agreement is for over three years then you must legally provide a written agreement. A typical tenancy agreement will include the length of the agreement, the rental income payable, if you can increase the rent and any obligations you and the tenant must abide by. As this legal document will form of the basis of your investment it is very important to get it right so I would advise to speak to a professional letting agent to draw this up. You can find some very good samples online but if I would advise to speak to a professional prior to handing over the keys.

How to Manage Tenants

When it comes to managing your tenants the best advice is to treat your tenant as you would like to treat. Landlords sometimes get a bad reputation but this is only a small minority, just like tenants it is also a small minority who cause major issues.

Management/Letting Agent vs Self-Management

A key decision you will have to make is if you are looking to hire a management agent to manage the day to day running of the property or if you will manage the investment by yourself. If you are looking to self-manage but you don't have time to find a tenant then you can pay for a professional letting agent to find and screen potential tenants which can be a great time saver.

Advantages of using management/letting agent

The key advantage of using an agent is it can often save you a lot of time and the person managing your tenants is a professional. This professional can take a lot of stress out of buy to let but it does come at a cost. As we have discussed there is quite a lot of legislation in place in regard to letting property so by paying a professional they can make sure you carry out of the necessary checks and provide a safe ongoing investment. The key word in this section is 'professional', there are some agents who are not above board when it comes to this sector so it is very important to make sure you are handing the keys over to a professional. A lot of landlords only use agents who are ARLA register (Association of Residential Letting Agents) or who are part of an ombudsman.

Disadvantages of using a management/letting agent

The major disadvantage is cost, if you just looking to find a tenant then this will usually be a fixed cost and if you are looking for a management service then you usually pay between 5-15% each month for the entire length of the tenancy (depending on the type of investment). When it comes to management agents having repairs carried out, in the past there have been horror stories of agents hiring very expensive workmen to carry out basic repairs and the landlord paying the bill. By being one step away from your investment you will not truly know what is going on and for some landlords this is not ideal.

Late Rental Payments

Late payment of rent is a direct breach of the tenancy agreement. Some naive landlords think it will never happen to them but most experienced landlords aim to factor in two months per year of not receiving rent (this could be because of a rental void or other factors out of your control). It is very important to remain calm if this happens because any over-reaction can make the problem worse and potentially lead to legal action against yourself (in the form of fines or even imprisonment).

The majority of late rental payments are down to admin errors (such as not having the correct amount of money in specific bank account on a certain day or late receipt of wages/housing benefit) and can easily be resolved. Or your tenant may have a reason for delaying the rental payment so I would always advice to try and settle the matter in an amicable way. If it has been a few days and your tenant has not been in touch then I would advise to post a letter detailing the rental payment is overdue and a few potential options (such a repayment plan).

If you hear no response from the initial letter then I wouldn't start to panic too much, your tenant may for example be on holiday or simply may not have had the time to respond. After 14 days of the late rental payment I would advise to send another formal letter explaining legal action may be taken against the tenant and guarantor if applicable.

If after 21 days of the late payment you still haven't heard anything, I would send a final letter to the tenant and also guarantor if there is one. If you still have no response I would start to worry a bit but remember to remain calm and professional and send a letter via recorded delivery to explain legal action will now be taken to repossess the property.

We will discuss evicting a tenant in the next section, but I think it is important to spell out some of the things you should never do as the following could lead to a fine or potential imprisonment.

You should never:

- Visit the property without prior consent from the tenant
- Cut off utility supplies
- Remove the tenants belongings
- Block access to the property
- Force a tenant to leave without legal action
- Act in any way that could considered threatening, this includes via telephone, email or social media

Eviction of Tenants

An eviction of a tenant should be the last resort as a landlord as it can be expensive, time consuming and very stressful but always remember the tenant is in breach a legal document and you have the legal right to remove them from the property. Under the 1988 Housing Act you can begin legal proceedings after non-payment of rent for two months (these two months can be spread over a length of time and do not need to be consecutive). You should begin by serving your tenant with a Section 8 Notice informing them a court case will be pursued if rent is not paid in the following 14 days.

If after 14 days you have no response then you can apply for a possession order which will give you the legal right to repossess the property. At this stage you will need to demonstrate how the tenant has breached their agreement and a possession order can be delayed or dismissed if you do not provide sufficient evidence or if you do not follow the correct process. If a possession order is granted then the tenant must be given 14 days to leave the property, with prior warning and the eviction must be carried out by a court-ordered bailiff in possession of a valid warrant.

If you ever find yourself in this position it is important to get legal advice as your scenario could differ slightly meaning a route to resolution could be different. The law can change so at the time of writing the previous discussed section are correct but can change at any time.

Managing Difficult Tenants

Buy to let should be seen as a long term investment, the majority of landlords and tenants just want an easy life however you if you let property for a long period of time then you may end up with a bad tenant. Probably the best piece of advice in regard to bad tenants is to try not to avoid them in the first place. Although this is easier said than done, we have discussed ways you can limit your risk but 'fail to prepare, prepare to fail' comes to mind. If you are using a letting agent then they will manage the day to day running of the property which can sometimes save you a lot of time and stress.

Your Responsibilities as a Landlord

Keep Your Property Safe

Your primary responsibility being a landlord is make sure your property is safe, you are providing a service and similar to any service you receive you would expect it to be safe and meet any applicable regulation. In this section will we discuss the necessities that are bare minimum but you may find other parts of the property which are not safe, such a carpets which are fitted properly or no hand rail on the stairs etc., this is where a letting agent can provide excellent advice to make your property safe and lettable.

Gas and Electrical Appliances and Safety Checks

As previously mentioned you will be responsible for the gas and electricity in the property. It will be your responsibility for a qualified and registered professional to visit the property at least every twelve months and carry out any work needed (you will also need to keep a records of this). If you are providing any appliances with the buy to let you will also be responsible for the safety of these devices also (for example any white goods, cookers, fridges etc.).

Smoke/Fire Alarms

This one is little known, but you if you have a standard buy to let you will need to have at least one fire alarm on each level of the property and one in the main living room/area of the home. If your property has an open fire/log burner then you will have a carbon monoxide detector in the property.

If you are looking to invest in a HMO then you need to very careful with this one, if your property requires a license then it is important to adhere to the rules the license states, you will also need a fire alarm in the property, fire doors and a clear exit strategy in the event of a fire.

Carrying out Repairs

As part of your day to day life as a landlord you will need to carry out repairs to the property, if these repairs are not sorted out quickly then they can sometimes escalate to more expensive ones. If you are ever having work carried out then it is important to ensure a professional tradesperson does this and you keep any receipts in the event of shoddy work.

Insurance

Sometimes the unthinkable can happen so it is important to have the correct insurance in place. I once heard of a landlord who did not update their standard residential buildings insurance to cover the property in the event it was let out. By not having adequate landlords insurance in place this individual was not covered and was stung with a hefty bill due to damage to the property and their insurance not paying out.

Buy to Let Tax

Rental Income

Rental income from buy to let is the same as receiving income from any other source; you may need to tax on this income. In order to pay tax (assuming you own the property in your personal name and not via a limited company) you will need to complete a self-assessment every year. As soon as you complete on a purchase for a rental property it is important you register with HMRC as being self-employed. If you are not using an accountant to do this, then every twelve months you will complete a self-assessment by 31st January every year, however the tax year runs from early April to the following April every year. For example if you completed a self-assessment in January 2017 then you will be providing your rental income (and any other income) to HMRC from tax year April 2015 – April 2016.

You will pay tax at 20% as basic rate tax payer, 40% as a higher rate tax payer or 45% as an additional rate tax payer. Tax can often change so it is very important to receive the correct tax advice from a qualified professional. To minimise the amount of tax you will pay you can offset some expenses, for example: interest on mortgage (please see below), management/letting fees, council tax, buildings insurance, ground rent, service charge etc.

Stamp Duty

As of April 2015, if you are looking to purchase a buy to let property or a second home you will pay an additional 3% in stamp duty on top of the normal charge. This measure was brought in to try and curb the amount of people of people who are looking to enter the market. This tax is payable for any property purchase where you are not replacing your existing home, so for example if you are looking to let out your existing residential property and then purchase a new home the tax is payable. It is worth mentioning that you will have a 36 month window where this can be refunded, so if for example you let out your existing home when buying a new place you will have the option to sell your previous home within the 36 month window and the additional stamp duty paid will be refunded. Please see below a chart which shows how much additional tax you may have to pay.

Band	Existing residential SDLT rates	New additional property SDLT rates
£0* - £125k	0%	3%
£125k - £250k	2%	5%
£250k - £925k	5%	8%
£925k - £1.5m	10%	13%
£1.5m +	12%	15%

Tax Relief on Mortgage Interest

Another big change in buy to let tax is that mortgage interest will gradually become non-deductible as a business expense. Prior to tax year 2017/18 you were able to treat mortgage interest or loan interest as a business expense, meaning you would pay tax on your rental income, minus mortgage interest and other expenses, however starting tax year 2017/18 you start the pay based on the entire rental income you receive. If you own a buy to let property which is mortgage free this will not affect you, the changes will only impact those who have mortgages or loans secured against a property.

Below is a chart which details the amount of interest you will be able to deduct from your overall rental income. As we can see the changes will be implemented over a four year period, which by the tax year 2020/21 you will not be able to deduct any interest as a tax liability.

Tax year	Percentage of interest deductible from rental income
2017 – 2018	75%
2018 – 2019	50%
2019 – 2020	25%
2020 - 2021	0%

There a few exceptions to the new tax rules, the main one being if you purchase/own your property through a limited company you will still be able to claim this tax relief. Although as previously discussed, this is quite a niche area when it comes to mortgage lenders, in the coming years this may become more mainstream as mortgage lenders do have an appetite for lending.

The other key exception is for furnished holiday lets, if you proceeding down the holiday let route then could be a very good way of getting around the tax.

Wear and Tear Allowance

In recent years wear and tear allowance used to be a great tax advantage of buy to let, you used to be able to claim 10% of net profits as a deduction due to wear and tear of furniture in the property (if your property is let on a furnished basis). As of tax year 2016/17 the rules have changed. You can still claim against wear and tear however it has to for replacement items in the property, not the initial purchase. For example if you buy a table and chairs for a new buy to let property you will not be able to offset this cost against tax, however in a few years if you need to replace a chair then you can deduct this cost against your tax liability. I would always recommend keeping an up to date inventory and any receipts in case HMRC question the expense. It is also important to note furnished holiday lets are given their special tax treatment so you will be able to claim against the standard wear and tear allowance.

Capital Gains Tax

When it comes to selling a buy to let property you may be liable to pay capital gains tax, this tax is essentially payable if you sell an investment property for a higher amount than you originally paid for it. If you own the property in your personal name (not via a limited company) then you will have a £11,000 annual allowance you can use to offset this tax. Depending on your income and any capital you may already have you will either pay 18% or 28%. There are ways in which you can reduce this tax bill, for example:

- Estate agent / solicitor/ selling fees of the property
- Stamp duty
- Any loss you may have made in previous on another buy to let property

If you have ever lived in the property you are selling then you may be able to reduce capital gains tax, but it important to speak to a qualified tax adviser or accountant who will be able to provide advice.

At the moment if you owe any capital gains tax from the sale of a property then you must pay this by the following January, so for example if you sold a property in June 2017 then you must pay the tax by January 2018. As of 2019 you will need to pay this tax within 30 days of sale

Insurance Available for Landlords

A type of insurance I would thoroughly recommend and may be compulsory from your mortgage lender is landlords insurance. This insurance is very similar to standard residential insurance for your home but is specifically designed for landlords. The insurance will pay out in the event of flood, fire etc. and as mention I would thoroughly recommend it. If you only have standard buildings insurance in place and the insurer finds out you are in fact letting the property then there is chance they may not pay out. When you take out a policy you may be given the options to cover rental income, legal expenses in the event of eviction and other scenarios. The level of insurance you decide to take out will depend on the level of risk you are willing to take and how this will impact your monthly profit.

Chapter 4 – Glossary

Accident, Sickens and Unemployment Cover - A policy which pays out if you are unable to work due to an accident, sickness or if you are made unemployed

Advance – Amount of mortgage/loan

AST – Assured shorthold tenancy agreement

ASU – Accident, Sickens and Unemployment Cover

Base Rate – Usually refers to the Bank of England Base Rate

Bridging Finance – A short term loan usually used to purchase a property quickly

BTL – Buy to let

Capital gains tax – Tax payable on sale of an asset which is calculated on the original purchase price paid in comparison to the sale price

Capital raising – Borrowing additional funds above the mortgage balance needed for the property (for example, borrowing extra for home improvements).

Capped rate – A variable which is guaranteed to rise above a certain rate (a ceiling)

CGT – Capital Gains Tax

Collar – A minimum rate you will pay on a variable rate mortgage

Completion – When a property purchase is complete and if applicable the mortgage begins

Conveyancing – Legal work done by a solicitor for a purchase or remortgage

Corporate let – A property let to a company

CTL – (Consent to let) when a mortgage lender allows you to let out a residential property

Debt consolidation – Incorporating debt into a mortgage (for example credit cards, loans etc.)

Deed of postponement – Delaying a second charge loan on a property

Deposit – The amount you money you out down towards a property

Discount variable rate - A rate which discounts a lenders standard variable rate and is not linked to Bank of England Base Rate

EA – Estate agent

Early repayment charge - exit fee to leaving a mortgage deal early (for example remortgaging in the middle of a 5 year fix with ERCs)

EPC – Energy Performance Certificate

Equity – the percentage of a property you own, for example if you own a property worth £100,000 and you have a mortgage of £80,000, you will own £20,000 in equity.

ERC - Early repayment charge, the exit fee to leaving a mortgage deal early

Exchange of Contracts – When a purchase becomes legally binding

Fixed rate – Fixed rate of interest for fixed period of time (for example 2, 3, 5 years)

Flipping property – Purchasing and renovating a property with the intention to sell the property for a profit

Freehold – When you own the land as well as a property

Freeholder – A person who owns the freehold for a property

FTB – First time buyer

FTL – First time landlord

Gazumped – Losing a property due to being outbid or a cash buyer decides to buy the property

Gazundering - When a person looking to purchase a property offers a lower amount, usually at the end of the process of buying a property

Ground rent – Money you pay to a freeholder usually for a leasehold property

HMO – House of multiple occupations, a property that is usually let on multiple tenancy agreements

Interest only – You only pay interest on the mortgage balance, if you do not make overpayments, the mortgage balance will stay exactly the same

Interest rate – The amount of interest you will pay for a mortgage/loan

Joint borrower, sole proprietor – One person named on the deeds whereas two people are named on the mortgage

Let agreed – a tenancy has been agreed

Let to buy – transferring your existing residential home into a buy to let and then purchasing a new residence

Letting agent – A company which finds and assesses eligibility of finding a tenant

Loan to Value – The value of a property in comparison to a mortgage or loan, for example a property valued at £100,000 with a £60,000 mortgage would have a loan to value of 60%

LTV – Loan to Value

Management Company – A company which specifically works to manage the day to day running of a property.

Negative Equity – When a mortgage balance is higher than a property's value

No ERCs – A mortgage deal that has no exit fees, you will be able to clear the entire mortgage balance through remortgaging or paying the entire mortgage off

Offset – A facility on a mortgage which links to a bank account where funds can be deposited, you will not benefit from interest on the funds deposited; however you this will limit the amount of interest you will pay on the mortgage. For example your mortgage balance is £200,000 and you deposit £50,000 into the offset account, you only pay interest on £150,000

Overpayments – Paying more than the minimum monthly mortgage payment in order to reduce your mortgage balance quicker

Portfolio - A group of properties an investor owns

Property Chain – simultaneous buying and selling of properties

Redemption – Paying back a mortgage balance early

Releasing equity – Borrowing more money above your current mortgage balance in order to purchase a property, for home improvements or any other reason

Remortgaging – Using a new mortgage to repay your existing mortgage and in order to usually benefit from a lower interest rate or secure additional borrowing

Repayment mortgage – You pay both interest and capital every month and at the end of the mortgage term the entire balance will be cleared

Secured debt – Debt which is secured against a property for example a mortgage

SPC – Special Purchase Vehicle

SSTC – Sold subject to contract, a property where the vendor has agreed to sell their property

STLT – Stamp duty land tax which is a tax payable on the purchase of a property

Studio flat – A small flat usually with a shared living room/bedroom

SVR – Standard variable rate

Term – The length of time a mortgage is taken over (for example 25 years)

Tracker rate – Interest rate that is set above or below the Bank of England Base Rate

Unencumbered property – A property that is mortgage free (i.e. no debts are secured against the property

Unsecured debt – A form of credit that is not secured against the property

Valuation – When a mortgage lender values a property

Valuation fee – The fee you pay for a lender to value a property

Valuer's comments – A term used by mortgage lenders when a valuer is assessing if a property if adequate security

Printed in Great Britain
by Amazon